CONCILIUM

Religion in the Seventies

CONCILIUM

Religion in the Seventies

Volume 61: Dogma

SACRAMENTAL RECONCILIATION

Edited by
Edward Schillebeeckx

Herder and Herder

The Seabury Press
815 Second Avenue
New York, N.Y. 10017

Library of Congress Catalog Card Number: 76–129760
ISBN: 0–8164–2517–5
Printed in the United States

CONTENTS

PART III
DOCUMENTATION CONCILIUM

Editorial

AS systems of value change, the sense of guilt changes with them. Shortcomings in the private sector are regarded by many as of less importance than misdeeds which affect a wider sphere. In particular, the persistence of wars, armaments, colonialism or racialism arouses an intense sense of guilt in the younger generation. Within the Church, the change in the sense of guilt is manifested by a greatly diminished interest in the existing forms of the forgiveness of sins. Hence this number of *Concilium*, which is concerned with the "sacramental administration of reconciliation", begins with a sociological consideration of the connection between the sense of guilt and the cultural setting of those affected (Remy). If effective forms and rites of forgiveness are to be developed, this cultural context must be clearly known and taken into account. On the theological level, this necessity becomes apparent when one notes that sacramental forgiveness presupposes an *efficacious* sign. When a rite has lost all real significance, it ceases to be a sign. The faithful will quickly lose interest in such rites, when they ask themselves more clearly what they are doing. This theme is dealt with in the second article (Duquoc).

The emphasis which has been laid in recent centuries on penance or confession as the sacrament of the forgiveness of sins has often made us lose sight of the truth that the Eucharist is the great sacrament of reconciliation. The sacrificial meal, being a common social act, eliminates the self-centredness of sin. But this revaluation of the Eucharist as sacramental forgiveness of sins does not render a special ecclesiastical rite of forgiveness superfluous (Tillard). It is none the less necessary that the various local Churches should be given the possibility of developing their own rites in the matter. From the pastoral point of view, it cannot be right to impose uniformity, even in any given local Church. Time must be allowed for common acts of penance to be recognized as sacramental in the Church, as was done earlier for private confession (McCue). The various penitential liturgies of the Churches of the East actually show that common acts of penance are more primordial than private confession. The Churches of the West may well take notice of the practices of the East in order to overcome certain unbalanced features in the penitential liturgy (Nikolasch). And the penitential practices of the ancient Church also show marked differences as regards those of today. Personal confession of sins and the juridical aspect were less to the fore, while the common, social dimension was unmistakable. The function of the general priesthood of the faithful was recognized more clearly (Ramos-Regidor).

It has recently been said (Wicks) that Luther's position with regard to confession was his first clear departure from Catholic doctrine. McSorley makes an ecumenical contribution by showing that Luther's position was accepted by various fathers at the Council of Trent. The declarations of Trent on the integrity of the confession of sins in penance simply affirmed the necessity of it in certain circumstances. This is to be interpreted within the particular cultural context of the Council of Trent (Peter).

The bibliographical contribution explains why the Churches of the Reform were so reserved in their attitude to private confession. They were convinced that forgiveness of sins was not linked with the sacrament of penance. And they had their own views on the nature of the ministry or priesthood (von Allmen). Then follows a survey of the literature on penance published in the last ten years (Funke).

PART I
ARTICLES

Jean Remy

Fault and Guilt in the Perspective of Sociology*

Introduction

THE object of this article is to provide an instrument of sociological analysis by which to make a more systematic investigation of certain social facts, starting from such spontaneous experiences as the consciousness of guilt, pardon and reconciliation. We shall therefore start with guilt in the ordinary sense of the term and consider it as a category of perception, prescinding from the technical developments of psychoanalysis where conscious guilt in particular is contrasted with unconscious guilt. None the less, by a procedure different from that of the psychoanalyst, we shall bring to light the unconscious processes on the basis of which the conscious orientations are worked out. To do this we shall ask ourselves what are the links maintained by spontaneous perception with the social structure. We shall thus make a deliberate effort to make a non-normative analysis of a phenomenon which is experienced as normative. We shall not be concerned with analysing the meanings known to or experienced by the subject. We merely start with them and then go on to try to understand how these meanings are structured and what are their consequences in social life.

We shall thus examine in succession how guilt supposes an individualization of responsibility, and thus becomes a way in

* Part of some studies on the cultural impact of religion, carried out under the auspices of the Centre de Recherches Socio-Religieuses de l'Université Catholique de Louvain, with the collaboration of Liliane Voye, Francis Hambye and Emile Servais.

which cultural schemas are institutionalized. We shall then see how the sense of guilt is reinforced by the processes of pardon and reconciliation, the efficacy of which is linked with the existence of a mentality which lays stress on the value of harmony in common life. The examples cited in the course of this study aim at subjecting various experiences to this method of analytical inquiry, in order to verify the basis of the method and hence bring about a possible reappraisal of the instrument in question.

Though we try in this study to confine ourselves strictly to proposing the viewpoint of sociological analysis, we always remain conscious of its limitations.

I. The Socio-cultural Function of Guilt

A. INSTITUTIONALIZATION AND THE PERSON

1. *Reactions internal to the person*

Guilt appears when one has the sense of failure with regard to an image of oneself to which an emotional value has been attributed. Thus it need not appear when there is a gap between the explicit and the implicit image which guides our behaviour. One can, for instance, uphold verbally a certain conception of family life and behave in fact along other lines which are affectively chosen. The model defended verbally corresponds to a concern for collective justification. Disregard of it does not give rise to a sense of guilt. The same thing occurs in the life of the Church. Here some may be found to take a certain theology as the basis of their utterances, while actually organizing their pastoral options according to a different latent image. But this does not cause a sense of guilt. Thus our definition rejoins that of Laplanche and Pontalis, where guilt is linked to an affective state, resulting from an act which the subject holds to be reprehensible.[1]

It is interesting to note that this downgrading of one's image of oneself does not necessarily imply, directly, the relationship to another. One can, for instance, meet persons who feel guilty because they cannot keep to a diet in the interests of their health. Here the image of the self has taken on such a degree of autonomy

[1] J. Laplanche and J. B. Pontalis, *Vocabulaire de la Psychoanalyse* (Paris, 1968), pp. 440–41.

with regard to the social context that the subject may try to maintain it in spite of the negative reactions of the group. However, if this process of self-determination is pushed too far, the image of oneself and the regions to which it assigns guilt can lead to a breakdown of communication. This seems in fact to be one of the elements which distinguishes a "pathological" from a "normal" sense of guilt. The former leads to a rupture of communication, while the latter sends one back to it. But in any case, this sense of guilt is operative only when the norm has been interiorized, and adopted by the person in function of this image to oneself. This image of oneself is, we hold, to a great extent a social construction.

2. *The return of the person to the system of group expectations*

We shall not delay here over the process by which this interiorization comes about or the very special functions which are fulfilled by the "significant others", that is, by the persons who are significant for the subject and are instrumental in his construction of his identity. Our aim is rather to go beyond a psycho-sociological orientation, to examine the collective functions fulfilled by the sense of guilt.

Guilt results from nonconformity with the image of self. But an essential component of this image is the organization of the relationship to others through the crystallization of a system of expectations which they hold in our regard. This statement may be illustrated by an example. In working-class circles, a good interiorization of norms will make the husband feel guilty if he does not give up all his wages to his wife. And his wife in turn, as she remarks his failure, may reproach him with it and find it astonishing if he is not ashamed of his behaviour. In middle-class circles, however, a similar relationship of mutual confidence is expressed through different norms. Thus relations with others take on concrete forms, according to the various social settings, which establish systems of expectations, rights and duties. And this set of foreseeable attitudes allows guilt to take shape by providing sure co-ordinates for any failures.

In this analysis, guilt appears as the *sense of an individual departure from the norms of the group*, even if this fact is not consciously perceived. On this basis guilt takes on, in a hidden

way, the *function of cultural reintegration*. This means that guilt is a mechanism which assures *institutionalization*, that is, the generalization of models of behaviour at the level of the group average, and the persistence of such models in time.[2] No doubt, the group disposes of other mechanisms, apart from guilt feelings, to assure the stability of behaviour and reactions. There is coercion or remuneration, for instance, in various forms. But in this case the efficacy depends essentially on the visibility of behaviour, while guilt, on the contrary, is based on interiorization. None the less, the various mechanisms are inter-connected. They are always more or less combined, with one or other of them predominating. Hence one finds that normally guilt predominates where institutionalization can be based directly on the potentialities of the system of the personality.

3. *Efficacy linked to the individualization of responsibility*

It follows that guilt, to be operative on the collective level, supposes an individualization of responsibility. If this link is to become concrete, it should be expressed through precise gestures of which the person can make himself master. And then these gestures will vary according to their setting in time, space and milieu. This means that the expression of the same fundamental demand will present us with different concrete indicators which in a given social construction will express guilt by other gestures. Thus, for instance, faced by the same demand for the respect of equality between men, some will feel guilty if they do not eat in the same room as their gardener, while for others the same sense will result when they have not taken part in some demonstration against a wrong.

However, it is not always easy to find simple gestures to give concrete form to responsibility. Further, it often happens that the absence of collective effort in this direction inhibits the development of a profound sense of guilt. It may well happen, for instance, that an employer feels himself hardly guilty at all when his treatment of his workers is incorrect, since his attitude has not been given concrete form in a set of socially defined gestures.

But it is not enough to assure the existence of guilt with regard

[2] J. Remy, "Innovation et développement des structures", in *Lumen Vitae*, XXIV (1969), no. 2, pp. 201–29.

to definite behaviour, as for instance through the exaltation of duty, if the value is to be affirmed. This could lead to a form of ritualism where security is found by clinging to concrete modes of behaviour which do not arouse reflection. The individualization of responsibility supposes that the subject perceives an effective relationship between the precise gestures which he can furnish and the value to be pursued. Otherwise there is the danger that he will be demoralized, or find that it is unimportant to conform to these gestures. In such a situation, guilt may attach to other spheres of collective life. This may happen, for instance, when the subject perceives a disproportion between the collective aim, such as aid for the underdeveloped countries, and his own individual possibilities. So too the social neutralization of a value takes place through the enfeeblement of the concrete actions which support it.

It follows that the integrating function of guilt is all the more assured the more strongly it is mediated by a sense of failing others and the more this failure is seen in terms of gestures within the reach of the individual but not accomplished by him, since he has failed on the level of quality of intention and generosity. Hence when a group relies mainly on the mechanisms of guilt feelings to assure conformity, it must lay stress on a collective interpretation where the quality of social life is seen to result from a number of interpersonal relationships sustained by the generosity of each individual.

It should not however be deduced from what has been said that guilt, as a regulatory mechanism, functions only in interpersonal relationships. It has a much wider scope and takes in all behaviour which is experienced as within the control of the person. It is possible to have guilt feelings for having filled in one's income tax returns incorrectly.

4. *Reassurance and collective guilt*

Individual guilt feelings, such as have been discussed above, take on the character of reassurance for the person. Through the concrete form taken by the required behaviour, guilt allows one to dominate the anxiety of a situation of uncertainty. There is an old formula of catechetics which may be quoted here with a slight

modification: "Only a saint can confess every day without being a neurotic".

Collective guilt, however, leads to the opposite result. It undermines security and becomes demoralizing in the long run, since it downgrades the positive image which the group has of itself, while not giving individuals the feeling that they can transform it, at least at once. In the matter of law and order, for instance, one may experience a profound disquiet at the end of certain cases where justice is impotent with regard to certain problems. When this happens, either the misgivings in question must be neutralized by collective steps or they will result in demoralization where no clear possibility of a rapid collective transformation can be envisaged. To avoid such demoralization the group can also turn to symbolic purifications. The effort to assign blame and responsibility allows the group to throw off its sense of insecurity, by the effort to individualize the fault. This seems to be the meaning of certain rites of purification such as may be seen in the MacCarthyism of the United States after the Russians had launched their first satellite.

Hence the members of a group cannot continue to identify with it through a negative image. Individual guilt feelings may be an efficacious stimulant for an effort of readjustment, but this is not true of collective guilt. Faced with such loss of security, the group has various procedures for re-establishing equilibrium. No analysis in depth can afford to ignore them.

None the less, our previous findings lead us to think that guilt is rather a mechanism for the reintegration of the individual into the group than a procedure by which the objectives of the group are transformed. On the group level, guilt can intervene only indirectly, as we shall further show in our analysis of social movement.

5. *Institutionalization and orientation of induced guilt feelings*

The link between guilt feelings and the process of institutionalization leads to the creation of a sensitivity to faults which differs from one domain to another. The demands of the social order, for instance, have to be related to the order of priorities which is menaced by the disorganizing impact of the individual rupture. Thus, the average members of the group have to be

protected from the effect of breaches of order which they may note either in domains felt to be decisive for the future of the group or in domains where there is a risk of nonconformity becoming the general position. For instance, in a society where family morality is felt to be the basis of the social order, the parish will take up a strict attitude towards a father of a family known to be lax in sexual matters, while it will be less severe as regards the shameless way in which the same man treats his employees in the management of his business. So, too, Catholics can feel themselves more guilty for having broken off with Protestants than for taking part in certain types of social ascendancy. Thus guilt expresses a hierarchy of priorities and helps to reduce and express certain social conflicts while others remain less apparent or may even be denied as non-existent.

If these analyses are correct, the concrete forms of guilt and hence of moral feeling derive to some extent from criteria whose origin is not explicitly known to the person and which contribute, in a hidden way, to stabilize a social order by working out a system of evidences.

B. THE BREAKDOWN OF CULTURAL INTEGRATION THROUGH THE CREATION OF DIFFERENT TYPES OF GUILT

The dominant guilt feelings reflect, as we have seen, an order of priorities and relationships of power which social movement tries to challenge and change. We shall now offer some coordinates which may enable us to analyse this process of transformation, with regard in particular to this impact on guilt feelings.

1. *Absence of guilt feelings where such are expected*

The situation becomes grave for the established social order when the individuals no longer feel guilty in spheres where a strong sense of guilt was expected. These reactions may be viewed as pathological, and efforts will be made to apply such treatment to the individuals as will reintegrate them into group ways of thinking. But if the reactions in question become widespread, they may be the beginning of a cultural change with consequences hard to control, especially if the change takes the form of social movement.

Let us take the example of changes in the realm of sex. If a certain type of behaviour continues to be regarded as a shortcoming with regard to the norms, even when constantly repeated, a moral authority can lay the blame with human weakness and appeal to the generosity of pardon. It sees its role as reaffirmed throughout all its interventions. But when the sense of guilt weakens, while the authority may note that the moral sense is enfeebled, it has little power to bring people back to the right way. And from this juncture on, it may find that the foundation of its power is being undermined.

There was a striking situation of this type some years ago in Belgium, when the Court of Assizes at Liège acquitted a working-class mother of a family who had killed her child, the child having been born deformed as a result of certain medicines taken by the mother during pregnancy. I myself heard a number of women, of the working classes in particular, who said frankly that they did not know what they themselves would have done in the situation. The various authorities who then spoke out in favour of the right to live, including the religious authorities, were often criticized in these circles, and I can recall one reaction which seemed to sum up very well the feelings of the group: "The bishops have proved it again. They are on the side of the bourgeois. In the lower income groups, to have deformed children means that the poor cut themselves off from every chance of doing well. They are in a society which is very hard on its non-productive members. Why did the bishops not remind everybody that society is not doing its duty?" Basically, the pronouncements of the hierarchy had been regarded as a juridical reminder of the right to life, in a formalist perspective, with no effort being made to make "virtue" socially possible for all. The attribution of responsibility to *collective causes* released these persons from the sense of individual guilt and had the further effect of legitimating accusations against authorities who affirmed these principles lightly.

Thus this group read the situation in a way which was markedly different from the interpretation generally admitted. And the attitudes taken by the moral authorities seemed powerless to modify the reaction of this group. At the very most, these interventions could raise certain doubts, bring about a more or less shameful conscience with regard to the reactions which were felt. It is precisely this type of shameful conscience which social movement, when deliberately launched, seeks to change into a sense of pride.

2. *Social movement and the proud consciousness of rupture*

Certain changes which have come about in recent years in groups of homosexuals may be taken as the starting-point of our considerations here. These groups, instead of feeling themselves on the fringe, sometimes achieve a sense of being the protagonists of forms of liberation. From having a shameful conscience, they pass thus to a sense of pride, proudly conscious of not being guilt-ridden according to the prevailing models, and of being sufficiently autonomous to bring about this rupture with regard to the institutionalized models, which are regarded as repressive. This rupture is only possible through a social movement which is inspired by a strong affective mobilization and is therefore capable of creating an enthusiasm and an image which are very positive, even though associated with types of behaviour which are still generally perceived as deviate.

To be successful, the social movement must provide its members with a milieu with which they can identify. This explains why they readily adopt a language very like that of religion, and why mutual relationships are interpreted very intensely in terms of confidence, abandonment and possibly even treason. By means of this strong affective identification, new zones of guilt feelings are created. If the movement succeeds on the social level, these zones will tend in turn to spread throughout society slowly and progressively.

3. *Social movement as the base of cultural change*

When individuals or groups wish to modify zones of guilt feelings, it is not the best tactic to try to convince everybody of the validity of a reaction shared by a great number of persons. This approach supposes that a cultural change results from a series of conscious decisions, voluntary and well considered, as happens in the realm of technology when an innovation is adopted. In the cultural domain, evolution takes place in a very different way. Changes are due to collective movements which are relatively little reflected on, either as regards their origin or their orientation, and the efficacy of a social movement does not primarily depend on the organizations which it can make use of. No one can therefore be reproached with not having launched a social movement, though it may be right to reproach someone with not having founded, for example, an organization or association for charitable purposes. The social movement does more than change individual reactions. The whole power structure of a society begins to be transformed, since an opposing system is set up which disorganizes the hierarchy of objectives in the prevailing system.

4. *The ineffectiveness of appealing to the moral conscience without backing from the dominant culture*

We may take it, therefore, that the reference to the system of the personality is insufficient as the basis of an appeal to the moral conscience. To be effective, the appeal must also be based on the dominant culture. This is for instance what made it possible to create a sense of guilt in face of a phenomenon like the falling birth-rate, when spokesmen of the truth from their lofty chairs could appeal to each one's sense of responsibility and attribute the phenomenon to a lack of generosity. But the process did not bring about a new esteem for the large family. The mechanism had become inoperative because there were social mechanisms and a general mentality which imposed another norm imperative enough to eliminate the social effectiveness of the sense of guilt, whatever its force may have been, and to render it incapable of transforming the situation.

This example shows that preaching to the general public often owes its efficacy to the fact that it is in keeping with the dominant culture. It sees its power of creating institutions decline where it no longer corresponds to the latent cultural models which have evolved under the various collective pressures.

A connection of this type, which is normally not recognized by educators and not consciously experienced by their audience, functions independently therefore of the consciousness of those involved. It underlines the fact that the most effective of the social and cultural mechanisms are not those which are more clearly perceptible on the plane of spontaneous consciousness.

To return to the example of preaching, one may say that its link with the dominant culture is all the stronger when it strives to address the average members of the group. Its contacts would be somewhat different if it was aimed at persons who belonged to collective movements of "contestation". Here the appeal to the moral conscience could intervene as a mechanism amplifying the collective statements which these movements are trying to articulate and promote, as against the dominant culture. And these movements, at such moments of great collective risk, are in need of intellectual analyses which will enable them to regain forms of security.

This difference of meaning poses an important problem for the action of the Church. Can it be right to treat all Christians as if their collective situation placed them all well within a social movement? Should one not rather accept an internal pluralism and affirm that a tension between institution and innovation is the normal thing?

II. The Myth of Concord or Rupture as Guilt

A. SOCIETY AS A TENSION BETWEEN INSTITUTION AND INNOVATION

Society is, we think, a constant tension between institution and innovation, organization and social movement, dominant system and opposing systems which seek to impose another view of social priorities. At different times in the history of a society, sometimes institutionalization gains ground, sometimes innovation. This means that men have to face a changing set of problems. With this collective fact in mind, we try to analyse the social function of "imaginary concord".

B. THE MYTH OF CONCORD AND THE CATEGORIES OF PARDON AND RECONCILIATION

By the "social myth", we do not mean any sort of artificial or dangerous imaginary element, but the images and guide-lines which are more or less latent, which are accepted by the group and which it uses to imagine the ideal conditions of its collective life. Thus a social myth may be built up by means of concrete images drawn for instance from the sphere of family life. In this case, solidarity among all, realized at once, is one of the central focuses of socialization. Everyone then feels ill at ease if he is in profound and persistent disagreement with others. These disagreements, furthermore, are felt to be all the more guilt-laden the more they are interpreted as the result of bad will or of the poor quality of interpersonal relations. In this context, rites of pardon and reconciliation are readily established, to enable men to reaffirm the unity and profound solidarity of the group around its hierarchy of values. Pardon then appears less as a gesture than as a process of rehabilitation within which the recognizably guilty party must gradually make himself accepted once more.

C. LATENT FUNCTION OF THE MYTH OF CONCORD: INNOVATION AS GUILT

Reference to a myth of concord based on images drawn from the family may mean that conflicts inside the community are felt as more guilty than external ones. The Church seems to have, for instance, a theology of war definitely more developed than the theology which it has at its disposal to deal with conflicts within society in general, such as the struggle of the classes.

If this myth of concord is associated with an image of society regarded as a great organism where every element has its proper place—where the stomach should not try to exercise the functions of the heart, and so on—the reference to the dominant institutions is still more emphatic. In such a context, any struggle for power, any voluntary mobility in society, can only appear as aberrant. Images such as the notion of the Church based on the Mystical Body present a social group in the guise of an established order which is to be respected and which is to be the vehicle of the public good.[3] A theology of reconciliation can take a similar turn. Ideologically, it readily becomes a theology of conciliation and then easily becomes the tool of the dominant group.

As regards the sociological analysis, it is of little importance that such consequences are not deliberately sought by anybody. They are none the less operative. This is precisely what the

[3] To stop the foundation of the Jeunesse Œuvrière Catholique, the spokesmen of the Action Catholique de la Jeunesse Belge explained to the future Cardinal Cardijn that his initiative might loosen the bonds of the mystical body of Christ. See J. Meert, M. Fievez and A. Aubert, *Cardijn, sa vie et son œuvre* (Brussels, 1970).

sociologists mean by latent functions. They are consequences neither aimed at nor perceived by the agents, but which can be decisive in an evaluation of the phenomenon from the point of view of social effectiveness.

D. DISLOCATION OF THE FAMILY IMAGE IN GROUPS OF INNOVATORS

When some groups find themselves in permanent disaccord, their image and guide-line based on the myth of the family is dislocated, at least on the level of society as a whole.

Now, for various structural reasons, it is possible that our complex societies can have place for a number of internal oppositions, which may then be used by individuals to establish their own identity.[4] Such a situation of society would be the opposite of the traditional, which had little tolerance except for external opposition, one of the bases on which the collective identity was established. It may be these historical circumstances which explain why the theology of war was much more developed than a theology of conflicts within the community.

If this analysis is correct, the set of images provided by the family may cease to be of importance to many as a guide-line for thinking out the nature of society as a whole. Reconciliation based on a sense of short-term harmony loses its meaning for those who have a sense of a profound disaccord, seen as relatively long-lasting, and experienced perhaps as a condition for the formation of new values. The desire for reconciliation may then appear to them as a long-term objective, and also as not a gesture but a movement taking place progressively throughout many uncertainties. At this juncture, reconciliation no longer suppresses the conflict but in certain respects integrates it. There is short-term opposition, but men are patient with one another on the basis of long-term hopes.

This type of reconciliation may not be found acceptable whenever the zones of solidarity are felt to be very weak and the zones of opposition very intense. At a time of fierce opposition between guerrillas and land-owners, can there be much meaning in a common celebration of the Eucharist, even if the long-term hope

[4] J. Remy, "Conflits et dynamique sociale", in *Lumen Vitae*, XXIV (1969), no. 1, pp. 26–50.

is stressed? What meaning can the black American supporter of "Black Power" attach to a reconciliation with whites? Even if he enters on negotiations, the question of community seems to him, at least for the present, an inadequate statement of the problems.

Where the two image-myths coexist in collective life, a delicate social and cultural problem arises. The two groups find it difficult to agree on the fundamental categories of perception. This confusion could then bring about an attitude of withdrawal in many persons, who are bewildered by the different options. Here we see once more the problem of institutionalization, which tends to be the mainstay of the average member of the group—those who are not profoundly committed to one side or the other.

This social analysis is very important if one is interested in the latent functions which a "myth" of concord may exercise with regard to the dominant institutions and the movements of innovation. And then, the partial and multiple solidarities which are admitted by our complex societies may well weaken the operative character of a family "myth", at least if this ideal is regarded as aiming at a concord to be realized speedily.[5] As a consequence, the categories of reconciliation and pardon, and even the category of guilt, are in danger of losing their meaning—unless they happen to be used as the basis of blaming others rather than as a mechanism of personal reintegration.

III. Conclusion

In this article, we have confined ourselves to the investigation of the link between guilt and social structure, in the light of the tension between institution and innovation. But a complete analysis of the problem would also have to envisage the link between guilt and social effectiveness. This link seems to be based on the fact that social life is interpreted in terms of the good or evil intentions of the members of society. The criterion of its value is the quality of relationships between individuals. But if the human sciences, stressing the unseen and involuntary consequences of

[5] J. Remy and F. Hambye, "Crise de la Communauté situation provisoire ou changement culturel?" in *Lumière et Vie*, XVIII (1969), no. 93, pp. 85–112.

individual or collective gestures, make a non-moralizing interpretation of social life acceptable to the general public, there seems to be a danger that responsibility will not be analysed in terms of guilt but in terms of an incorrect analysis of a situation—as, for instance, when the risks involved are such that a failure necessarily follows. Now that the techniques of the human sciences are building up towards mastery of relations with others and of social interventions, without making use directly of the mechanism of guilt, it is no doubt important, from the point of view of a Christian evaluation, to react consciously and lucidly with regard to something which—perhaps in a hidden way—is at the origin of a new concept of individual and collective destiny. Such a reaction is necessary even if the human sciences are in this respect only taking their first steps. In any case, they should not be confused with utopias which claim to be guiding lines.

Such a reaction is all the more necessary since the analyses in question may well be applied to the internal life of the Church and could create in some an autonomy of judgment and reaction. We shall confine ourselves to posing, in the guise of conclusion, some questions inspired by this perspective.

Among other things, does not an acquaintance with these complex mechanisms make it possible to establish a form of reconciliation, that is, of the restoration of the individual in his totality and in his true relationship with his whole situation? The reconciliation would be full of meaning, inspired as it would be by a common hope, in a world dominated by decisions taken in uncertainty, where many short-term conflicts are the condition for the new creation. But in such a context, would not reconciliation imply a previous sense of fault and of pardon? All interventions, interpreted in terms of responsibilities, do not necessarily lead to determining or creating a sense of guilt. None the less, the inducing of guilt feelings could be centred on the necessity of social analysis and of all that is helpful for the correct determination of social interventions. When it is thus situated in the more comprehensive context of the collective dynamism, it is essential not to minimize the active role of guilt feelings, and also to see it in its true relation to other processes.

What is the position of the Church in this perspective? Does it seek to intervene only on the level of persons, making use of interiorization and hence of guilt feelings? Or is its intervention in social life regarded in a wider perspective? If so, what is the situation of the Church in terms of social movement? Even on the level of intervention with regard to persons, does it aim above all at the creation of a new identity in Christ? If so, its central concern is not to create a community for its ethical interventions, but a community "in the mystery" ("*mystérique*", as it has been termed by some French-speaking authors). Even in this perspective, can the Church disregard the possible impact of such a "community in the mystery" in stabilizing or thwarting institution or innovation?

Translated by Kevin Smyth

Christian Duquoc

Real Reconciliation and Sacramental Reconciliation

TODAY the word "reconciliation" enjoys a prestige in theology that for long it had lost. A biblical term, it is becoming a key-concept in theology, having the good fortune to serve as a link between the diverse fields of christology, sacramentality and eschatology. Christ is the minister of reconciliation; penance and the Eucharist are sacraments of reconciliation; the eternal Kingdom of God is reconciliation fulfilled.

The concept of reconciliation doubtless owes its current success to a sociological transformation of the Christian mind which (under influences that are not all biblical) is turning its attention more and more to the collective dimension of faith. The concept seems capable of bringing forward a truth hitherto perceived at the level of feeling, and it has the capacity to combine negative and positive elements. Negative: it brings down judgment on the world of our time, for if our world needs reconciliation this is because conflict, strife and hostility are still its constant components; and this situation, for Scripture, points to a radical evil, for hatred among men is the historical mark of enmity with God. Positive: the old world is falling apart, it is lost; the new world—brotherly and transparent—is imminent; in Christ it is already there; so that reconciliation is not only a hope or a utopia, it is being achieved here and now.

The concept of reconciliation is dynamic; it integrates the destructive past with a movement that abolishes it. It is a messianic concept; it incarnates in an authentic movement the most indestructible of all desires—peace and transparency.

Yet reconciliation is an object of suspicion owing to the forms it assumes in the Catholic Church, and notably owing to the celebration of penance.

Like all ecclesial data, reconciliation appears under two aspects. First, it is seen as an authentic movement of individuals and communities. "If, when you are bringing your gift to the altar", Jesus said, "you suddenly remember that your brother has a grievance against you, leave your gift where it is before the altar. First go and make your peace with your brother, and only then come back and offer your gift" (Matt. 5. 23–24). It is also celebrated in two sacraments, the Eucharist and penance. The first of these, through the sharing of bread, symbolizes not only the reconciliation to come, but offers thanksgiving for reconciliation already achieved; while the second points to man's current opposition to the movement of reconciliation of which Christ is the minister and shows his constantly ambiguous attitude with regard to this movement: forgiveness is a necessary dimension of our existence in history as we make our way towards ultimate reconciliation. These two sacraments come into the order of symbolism, and it is this symbolical character that upsets many believers.

Either they are superfluous, it is felt, or else they constitute an obstacle to evolution: superfluous, if reconciliation is already achieved; an obstacle, through their inefficacy, if reconciliation remains symbolic. Neither eucharistic participation, nor forgiveness, has any meaning in our historical struggle for reconciliation if its symbolic effectuation constitutes an alibi to rob it of all "revolutionary" force. Sacramentality has become historically the instrument employed by the Church to draw off the powerful challenge and realism of the biblical concepts.

The current indecision of Christians regarding the validity of a double-aspect in the Church explains, it seems to me, their uneasiness regarding the sacraments, and notably regarding penance.

I. The Current Problem: Forgiveness or Reconciliation?

The sacrament of penance, as it is practised today in the Catholic Church, gives rise to many reservations. There are fervent Christians, including priests and religious, who are unable to overcome their repugnance to its method of administration. There are many facile explanations of their allergy: the loss of a sense of sin, forgetfulness of God, distaste for prayer. But these explanations are unfortunately of too universal a kind to throw light on this particular phenomenon—for they would apply just as much to lukewarm believers who nevertheless experience no distaste for the existing forms of the sacrament of penance and often have recourse to them. It is precisely where Christianity is taken most seriously that repugnance to the sacrament of penance is most apparent. So we must seek out regional explanations before falling hopelessly back on the universal basics of belief or unbelief.

A clue will serve as a guide-line in our search for the causes of the allergy, and it is this: that believers most sensitive to collective phenomena and to social injustices are also the most hostile to the existing forms of penance. Militant Christians engaged in trades-union or political activities, or involved in the class-war, are the first to be infected by the allergy to sacramentality as it exists in the Church today. There is no question at all of indifference to God or to the Gospel of Christ, but in their daily fight for the setting-up of a less inhuman society, and in their political projects, the sacrament of reconciliation strikes them as either meaningless or ineffectual. A serious attitude to reconciliation as something to be effected here and now empties of its meaning reconciliation symbolized in the sacramental act.

The conviction that private penance is useless does not in any way call Christ's ministry of reconciliation into question. On the contrary, all effective reconciliation is seen by these Christians as an act of Christ. They are aware of the concrete quality of reconciliation, of its truth at the heart of conflicts. But private penance seems to them to suppress these conflicts artificially through the subterfuge of an inward guilt and forgiveness that have no bearing on the real conditions of life. The uselessness involved here is not the same as, though very near to, the one experienced by many Christians when faced with the inefficacy of sacramental confession and forgiveness to bring about a true transformation of their conduct and intentions. In the context of "private penance", then, there is again arising in the Church the everlasting debate about the relations between collective and political action, aimed at establishing justice, and ecclesial and sacramental reality. The problem assumes concrete form in the frequently noted fact that the more seriously a Christian takes the historical struggle for reconciliation the less he perceives the meaning of the existing forms of sacramental reconciliation. Is this situation the outcome of a misunderstanding? Or do the existing forms of private penance form an obstacle (to the detriment of Christian inspiration concerning reconciliation) to all effective struggle for historical reconciliation?

The answer to these questions will be hypothetical: the current emphasis in Christianity on the dynamic and future character of reconciliation robs forgiveness of historicism, reduces it to a private dimension, in short devalues it. Struggle, as the active and committed form of reconciliation, has pride of place. Forgiveness, seen as obsessed by the past, is an obstacle to the freedom required for political struggle. The shift of emphasis in reconciliation makes the sacrament of penance meaningless; the social import of forgiveness is underestimated. The idealism inherent in politically orientated Christianity easily fits in with an historical necessity of progress and fails to recognize the strength of the obstacles to reconciliation. It forgets the reality of the article of faith: Christ died for our sins.

This tendency to draw away from sacramental penance finds connivance on the objective plane in the private form of its current administration: juridicism robs forgiveness of its seriousness.

If this hypothetical explanation of the current abandonment of sacramental penance is correct, it would remain to show that Christian reconciliation necessarily includes forgiveness within its structure and meaning; that the social import of sacramental penance resides ultimately in the link it establishes between forgiveness and reconciliation in our history. This dimension requires that the forms of its symbolization in the Church should be ceaselessly defined and delimited by the meaning that is to be brought out.

II. Struggle as Reconciliation

Before establishing the link between forgiveness and reconciliation we must take note of the reasons for the falling-away from the sacramental form of forgiveness. Reconciliation is to come, it is a concept expressing the future of our history; here and now we are immersed in the class-war and injustice. Brotherhood, transparency, peace are no more than hopes; whenever they have a germ of reality, the reality is regional. Such hopes and micro-achievements are certainly sufficiently potent to inspire social struggle and give rise to messianisms. Reconciliation is first lived in its negative aspect: struggle. Those who resisted the Nazi regime were able to imagine a contrary universe, forged in the solidarity, brotherhood and justice of their effort. Today, in the Churches, small spontaneous groups, deeply committed and politically like-minded, are fighting for a Church to their image, purified of hierarchical and anonymous relations, a place of free expression. These communities are revolutionary in aims and status; they criticize a society governed not by justice but by the interplay of private interests. The systems within which we live, whether capitalism or Stalinist communism, form an obstacle to all true reconciliation—they allow us only to dream of it. Henceforth it is in the struggle against established violence that the promise of reconciliation, which has not yet happened, lies; celebrations, good intentions, patching-up through compassion, private remorse—all these engender inaction and bolster up the *status quo*.

To those who see our world as repressive and struggle effectively against it, the sacrament of penance will appear to confine reconciliation within an unhealthy and inward-looking return to the past. This type of believer will prefer the eucharistic celebration of reconciliation, where they can ratify in participation the actual brotherhood of the struggle and bear witness to a universal hope of unity. Militant and forward-looking reconciliation gives forgiveness less value—we do not know what collective meaning to find in it.

The private nature of sacramental reconciliation has encouraged a sometimes exclusive concentration on sexual faults. It has maintained a high degree of guilt-riddenness in this domain. For some Catholics sin seems identified with transgression in sexual matters. The frequently neurotic character of these faults and their almost inevitable repetition makes of confession a therapeutic of psychic appeasement of unconquerable conflicts. The popularization of psychoanalysis, whether this is a good thing or over-hasty, has convinced many Catholics of the arbitrary character of certain norms in the Church; so that a process of guilt-shedding is at work without accession to responsibility. Where traditional prohibitions are evaporating, neither the gaps in education nor the complexity of human relationships favour the perception of true guilt and true innocence in those for whom sin used to signify the transgression of a recognized law.

The combination of a positive criticism of the fictive nature of sacramental reconciliation, and an incapacity to find a foothold among the new norms, robs penance of its seriousness and tends to make us forget the irreplaceable function of forgiveness in the process of reconciliation. And now, before passing on to the study of sacramental forms, it remains for us to clarify the interlinking between forgiveness and reconciliation, for it is only with these links as a base that it is possible to show both the contingency of our penitential symbols and their irreplaceable significance.

III. The Link between Forgiveness and Reconciliation by Penance

The report on lines of orientation produced by the National Council of the French JEC in February 1970 tries to pinpoint the signification of religious practice on two levels—that of penance and that of the Eucharist. Here we are only concerned with penance. The relevant text runs as follows:

> To have a religious practice means, for example, to rediscover the meaning of confession—not the exercise that engenders guilt to the point of neurosis, but the act that signifies that we are never the victims of fatalism. To know that in the last resort everything depends on the use we make of our personal freedom; to be able to say to those we love that we have loved them badly, that we are dependent on them to rediscover our unity—what is there more liberating? To recognize that History is determined by the men who make it, and not otherwise; to admit that we are responsible for the unjust situation in the contemporary scholastic and social scene; to dare to proclaim that Manicheism in all its forms is deeply alienating—that, for us, is the meaning of confession [roneoed text, no. 3122, pp. 15–16].

This quotation situates very well the basis from which it is possible to talk about "penance"; namely, historical, personal and collective responsibility. Thus reconciliation through penance is a rejection of fatalism and a call to an action that assumes our mastery over the future. The text situates equally well the liberating effects of recognition of our sin, and points the way to not enclosing ourselves in our actions as if in some logic of inevitability. The recognition of sin is in this sense a condition of newness: it looks towards the future. It is nevertheless worth noting that the notion of recognition ousts that of forgiveness. Forgiveness comes from others or it is given to others. The text alludes to an awareness of responsibility but says nothing of the significance proper to forgiveness in human relations and in our relations with God. This silence is ambiguous: it implies either the decay of this problematic, or else it accepts its evidence. It seems in any case to reveal the uneasiness to which we alluded above and which manifests itself in an incapacity to give meaning to the act of forgiveness as such.

The act of forgiveness has both a social and a religious dimension. It has a function; it breaks the logic of evil; it introduces a new principle; it is creative. A short story by Jerzy Kosinski[1] throws light on the dialectic of evil. During the war an adolescent boy is the butt of a peasant family—the farmer horse-whips him and spits in his face for his amusement. One day a peasant's child dies of poisoning, and the ill-treated boy, measuring from the father's grief how much peasants love their children, thinks up a revenge for his humiliations—he will make the children swallow balls of bread concealing a hook. The first victim is a little girl. "I turned away so as not to see her face and forced myself to think only of the lash of her father's whip. As from that moment I could look my persecutors fearlessly in the face, even provoking their blows and ill-treatment. I felt no pain at all. For every stroke I received they were going to pay with a pain a hundred times worse than mine. Now I was no longer their victim; I had become their judge and their torturer. . . ." In spite of the peasants' magic spells "death persistently took its toll and the children continued to die." It would have been necessary for the boy,

[1] Jerzy Kosinski, *Les Pas* (Paris, 1969), pp. 59–60.

both victim and torturer, to forgive in order that the hellish circle could be broken. Reconciliation cannot be separated from forgiveness.

To imagine reconciliation without forgiveness is to reduce it to the category of the triumph of an ideology or the extermination of the enemy. What is to be reconciled in our history is neither doctrines nor ideologies nor objective antagonisms between classes, but men. Reconciliation, if it is to be genuine, must certainly take account of objective conditions. The plan of reconciliation would be a sham if it did not include in its realization the transformation of objective social relations. However, it would be illusory to suppose that objective revolutions come automatically. Many people accuse Christianity of idealism because it accepts, at the celebration of the same sacraments, people having objective antagonisms and contradictory opinions concerning the social order. In reality, by not enclosing itself within real and objective antagonisms, or, better, by not giving absolute value to the struggle for objective reconciliation at the level of economic and political relations, Christianity makes this struggle possible because it ceaselessly opens it up, at the symbolic level, to the overcoming of hostility by forgiveness.

The sacramental symbolism of reconciliation invites us to consider two things: first, that reconciliation at the level of objective and collective data is by no means the totality of reconciliation; and, second, that the struggle for reconciliation necessitates the actual presence of its end. In the first case, the symbol harks back to a radical evil which no objective transformation would be able to eliminate; only forgiveness positively integrates this evil with the experience and history of mankind. In the second case, the struggle for reconciliation gains experience of the end which it proposes for itself in the symbol. The "not-yet" which we arrive at only in the obscurity of the symbol inclines the struggle otherwise; it opens it up to a dimension that breaks its logic. Every day brings examples of the impasses in which the struggle is enclosed: whether it is the Vietnamese or the Arab–Israeli conflict, it is obvious that the solutions are at quite another level than that of war. Struggles bring about new relationships based on force, they do not automatically bring about reconciliation. Of their nature they engender domination. A Hungarian film-director, having taken part in the establishment of the People's Republic in Hungary, told French television that his anguish lay in his inability, once the revolution was accomplished, to bring the dialectic of violence to an end. This end is of another order. In this sense forgiveness, by breaking the cycle of sameness—in this case, violence—leads the way to a new creation.

The parable of the prodigal son shows us a God not of judgment or vengeance but of forgiveness. His son is alienated from him, refuses contact with his father, hurts him. This attitude calls for a similar response, that the father should reject his son, refuse any move towards him. Forgiveness creates a new relationship: the offending past itself becomes positive; the circle of "rights" is broken. All definitive reconciliation requires that the circle of judgment should be broken, if it is true that no man is innocent. The celebration of penance invites us, like God, to break this circle. At a deeper level it signifies that the new creation, absolute reconciliation, is not within our power, for we ceaselessly re-make that circle; our innocence is never pure enough to be creative. Thus in the celebration we acknowledge our sin all together; we acknowledge our smallness before God, by imploring his forgiveness in Christ.

IV. The Urgency of Reforming the Rite

The objections brought forward against the current form of sacramental reconciliation are not to be resolved at the level of theological meaning; the bringing to light of the immanent relationship between forgiveness and reconciliation does not answer all the questions. In fact the actual rites, the form of the sacrament of penance, are the concrete mediations of its meaning. We cannot take refuge in an appeasing theological meaning so long as this meaning does not become apparent in the rite. That would be to erect as solutions to our ecclesial problems the dualism between symbol and meaning; whereas it is necessary that the meaning should be immanent in the symbol used, that is to say in the sacrament as it is celebrated. Current uneasiness regarding the sacrament of penance derives from the dichotomy between the manner of celebration and the meaning of sacramental reconciliation.

The existing form, inherited from Irish missionary monasticism, robs sacramental penance of its social character and implies that forgiveness and reconciliation belong to an inner conscience. Moreover, it encourages the sentiment already too prevalent in our society that religion is a private affair. So the form of a sacrament does influence its meaning; and as things are now it obscures its true significance. The reform of rites is thus not an undertaking of secondary importance—it is the very condition of understanding what Christianity is about.

The purpose is clear; it is provided by the necessary link between forgiveness and reconciliation at the level of our true history. The sacramental symbol should make clear that forgiveness is a social function necessary to our history as it makes its way towards reconciliation; that particular reconciliations are a promise of the total reconciliation that is impossible as things are now; and that enmity between men has a source which can only be understood in the light of the Christian revelation of sin and of opposition to God. There is no facile recipe, in a cultural world in mutation, for bringing the symbolic gesture into accord with the meaning. A return to the ancient methods of penance could not be a solution; they were extremely harsh and suited a Christianity that was a persecuted minority. As soon as the Christian religion became the dominant religion, the religion of the people, it had to lower the level of its demands. The private form of penance corresponds to a minimal cohesion of the group. At that time it was accepted that participation in the Eucharist was no longer circumscribed by objective and collective norms. The mediation of the community was reduced to the minimum: the role of the priest as witness or sometimes judge of the individual conscience. Avowal or confession acquired a basic position.

Does this private form of penance represent a concession to a mediocre form of Christian life? Is it a sacred therapy to appease consciences that are incapable of making their own the evangelical demands? Or does it illustrate an obsession with legalism in our relations with God? Is the institution of confession for faults that do not stop the forward-march of the community ascribable to an unhealthy desire for purity? It is difficult to answer these questions. Nevertheless we may be sure that the drift of the sacrament towards a private form led to discerning the conditions of participation in the Eucharist as being outside the life of the community, that is to say outside reconciliation with men. The faults submitted to public penance in ancient times were directly concerned with the cohesion and witness of the community, whereas the faults submitted to private penance are not defined by their impact on the community and its cohesion but by a universal law whose abstract nature becomes all the more marked as it touches on data more immediately linked with community life, for it tends to remain silent on political and economic matters. Yet the law takes on a very concrete form in the interpersonal domain and notably in the sphere of sex. Transgression in matters of sexual morality assumes considerable importance, for not only can it be very precisely defined but it often causes emotional turmoil. Sins of omission in communitarian, social and political matters do not benefit by such precise definition nor by such immediate emotional reaction. Thus it came about that personal feelings and their disorders became very important elements in the criteria for participation in the Eucharist. The reconciliation celebrated in the sacrament of penance is first and foremost a reconciliation with oneself, which becomes the sign of reconciliation with God—this is a far cry indeed from the symbol advocated by the early Church, reconciliation with one's brother as the sign of reconciliation with God. The form of administration of the sacrament is not harmless: it favours one aspect of reconciliation. The private form favours reconciliation with oneself in the interior of one's conscience, sole seat of authentic relationship with God. Other human realities, and notably economic and political relationships, escape all interference from Christianity.

The current criticism of private penance derives from a very simple insight: that collective sins of omission produce crimes. Christians often participate without a qualm of conscience in the collective demands made possible by the power of technical and scientific methods. In the context of this proliferation of evil the sacraments appear insignificant. This situation invites us to a great creative effort in the liturgical domain—otherwise the seeming discrepancy between our history and the symbolic celebration of reconciliation will grow; sacramental reconciliation will be seen as factitious, and be abandoned, or it will appear politically as a structure upholding the *status quo*. Hence the urgency of discovering new forms of celebration—not only in the West but in countries with old non-Western cultures. The rites passed on by our history were imposed on it without sufficient attention being paid to local forms of possible signs of reconciliation. Certainly efforts are being made today to extricate Christian sacramentality from the situation in which it finds itself. Up till now these efforts have not amounted to much—they have combined a public penitential liturgy with private confession. The gap between reconciliation with oneself and reconciliation with mankind, sign of reconciliation with God, is far from being overcome at the level of symbol. Confession still seems too bound up with an abstract law.

Yet I do not think we need despair. The current criticism of the insignificance of the sacrament of reconciliation spurs us on to new discoveries. The Church cannot for long do without an effective symbolization of the social, historical and collective function of forgiveness. The sacrament is not made only for the individual. Its collective meaning must shine forth from the liturgy. God's initiative of forgiveness cannot for long be confined within the private conscience—it is a creative force for our history. Wherever forgiveness is achieved, God is there.

Translated by Barbara Wall

Jean-Marie Tillard

The Bread and the Cup of Reconciliation

A CRITICAL examination of the gospels in search of the very pivot of salvation, the heart of the Christian confession of faith, inevitably ends up at the following words of St Paul: "Therefore, if any one is in Christ, he is a new creation; the old has passed away, behold, the new has come. All this is from God, who through Christ reconciled us to himself and gave us the ministry of reconciliation; that is, God was in Christ reconciling the world to himself (*kosmon katallasson eautò*), not counting their trespasses against them, and entrusting to us the message of reconciliation.... We beseech you on behalf of Christ, be reconciled to God. For our sake he made him to be sin who knew no sin, so that in him we might become the righteousness of God" (2 Cor. 5. 17–21).

Although it is difficult to explicate the last verse of this passage, and although exegetes have, especially since the Reformation, offered conflicting interpretations, Christian tradition as a whole is united in the major affirmation (brought out with splendid emphasis by Chrysostom[1]) that the mystery of Christian faith turns on a "reconciliation" arising from the wholly gratuitous love of God and manifest within the world in a humane brotherhood of those who are "reconciled" with one another. The first chapters of Ephesians depend on the same understanding of the essence of revelation: God's mystery opened forth. The grand design hidden from all eternity in the silence of the Father intends not merely communion (*koinonia*), in the same sense of

[1] *In Epist. II ad Cor.*, hom. XI, 2–3 (*PG* 61, cols. 475–9).

men united in love, but (and here redemption is seen as essentially connected with the purpose of creation) a communion and a human brotherhood of those inescapably characterized by a law of enmity and a fatal flaw setting them against God and against other men, and conducive to division even within the individual's inmost self (Rom. 7. 15–23). This threefold conflict expresses the profound and continually manifest reality of sin. Therefore reconciliation and *koinonia* must go together in God's realistic plan for men. The very essence of the second is primarily related to a transcending of, a victory over, sin. It is a *koinonia* in the reconciliation offered by God; and attains to its proper reality only by means of constant reference to its source and location—Jesus' paschal humanity. And Jesus' humanity was offered on the cross as a "propitiation" for the sins of men (Rom. 3. 25; 1 Jn. 2. 2, 4. 10), and exalted in the resurrection as the first fruits of the new world (1 Cor. 15. 20–3; Col. 1. 18). In the very flesh of the Lord, the Father offers those who will receive him the possibility of new life, open to God and open to other men, thus overcoming the confinement to which man is continually sentenced by sin. The openness of *new life* which, in Jesus, shows forth the dynamics of salvation itself must, by the action of the Holy Spirit, become manifest for the faithful Christian in his actual existence, so that it is opened out in a way wholly conducive to full reconciliation. In this way the Church is born; and St Paul (aptly, in this perspective) describes the Church as the body of Christ. Day after day, the Church is built up through the action of the Spirit; and, without remission, the Spirit plucks it out of sin in order to lead it towards the truth of actual reconciliation.

I. The Lord's Supper: Sacrament of "Reconciliation"

Understood in the light of the foregoing, the few texts of the New Testament which make explicit reference to what we now call the Eucharist are profoundly homogeneous. They all tend to affirm that when the Church is joined together for the Lord's Supper, it celebrates in thanksgiving and supplication the mystery of its own reconciliation. Admittedly, this reconciliation was accomplished once and for all (*ephapax*) in the event of the death-and-resurrection of Christ, but once again it is applied to the

Church, *hic et nunc*, in its sinful situation, by virtue of the sacramental character of the celebration and meal. By one and the same action the Church is freed from its sin and enters into a more authentic *koinonia*.

The Lord's Supper is a sacramental memorial. Regardless of whether the Last Supper coincided with an actual passover meal, the accounts of the institution of the sacrament evidently direct us to this interpretation, if only because of the words Paul and Luke attribute to Jesus: "Do this *eis tèn emèn anamnèsin*" (1 Cor. 11. 24–5; Lk. 22. 19): that is, "in remembrance of me". The Greek of the gospel traditions is a translation of the Hebrew *zikkaron*, a term with very precise connotations. In the liturgical context (obviously the case here) it characterizes a cultic act by which a past salvific event is recalled—but in order to relive *hic et nunc* the grace of that event in praise and blessing, which revives hope in the ultimate accomplishment of that salvation at the very moment when God is reminded of his promise and asked to realize it. There is no question of a purely subjective recall—a mere quickening of the believer's memory; what is implied is an objective reality by virtue of which the very effectiveness of the great events of salvation remains present throughout history. In the paschal meal, for example, under the signs of food and the community about the table, the present generation participates in the significant action of the first Easter. The axis of remembrance is this reality, which appears as a pledge from God re-encountered through the mediation of signs. In this way, the everlasting fidelity of God towards his people, and the irrevocable efficacy of the salvific events, continue to enliven those who receive them in faith and hope.

What exactly is the divine action which is thus connected with the Lord's Supper? It is the act of *reconciliation*. According to the words of the gospel narratives themselves, the bread that is broken bears the body given for all (Lk. 22. 19), the cup offers the blood of a covenant (Mt. 26. 28; Mk. 14. 24) which is the new covenant (Lk. 22. 21; 1 Cor. 11. 25), blood poured out for many for the forgiveness (*eis aphesin*) of sins (Mt. 26. 28). All these connotations are entwined in the very reality of the reconciliation that Jesus effected. Jeremiah might be said to have affirmed the characteristics of the new covenant in language based upon the experience of renewed friendship with but one ultimate cause: the fact that God would forgive crimes and forget sins (Jer. 31. 31–4). At the eucharistic meal, the Church is assured that in the signs of remembrance, by the power of the Holy Spirit alone, the body and blood of reconciliation are truly present to it, not merely so that the Church may fittingly praise God but above all so that it may participate once and for all (*ephapax*) in reconciliation. The Church is able to participate in this way by eating the bread and drinking from the cup of salvation. The significance of the latter above all is clear: by joining himself with the blood shed in forgiveness of sins, each believer is made part of the dynamism which we recall, and, reconciled with God, finds in communion through the power of the Lord's *agapé* the necessity and possibility of a life of reconciliation with his brothers, whoever they may be—an existence of due profundity.

This allows a better understanding of 1 Cor. 10. 16–17: "The cup of blessing which we bless, is it not a participation in the blood of Christ? The bread which we break, is it not a participation in the body of Christ? Because there is one bread, we who are many are one body, for we all partake of the one bread." The participation—the *communion*—does not come about merely by virtue of the fact that one, unique "body of Christ" is given to all: it originates in the reconciliatory power enclosed in that body. Just as in its paschal meal, generation after generation, Israel entered into communion with the efficacy of the salvific action carried out at the fringe of its history, so in their eucharistic meal the new people of God open themselves to the redemptive and reconciliatory power of the Lord's Passover. Through its major witnesses and in its various liturgical forms, tradition has never ceased to assert that at the Last Supper the Church derived its unity from participation in the nature of the unique event of Jesus' sacrifice of his life "in order to unite the divided and scattered children of God."

Considered thus in the perspective of its foundation, the Eucharist is the sacrament of ecclesial reconciliation. In the tracery, so difficult to arrange appropriately, of scriptural allusions to what one might call the mystery of forgiveness in the Church, baptism and the Lord's Supper stand out clearly as the two most prominent sacraments. Even though a comparative analysis of the documentation on the Eucharist and of the major texts relating to baptism (above all Rom. 6. 2–11; Col. 2. 12–13; Tit. 3. 5–7; 1 Pet. 3. 21–2) shows that these sacraments are both grounded in the same *ephapax* of paschal reconciliation, it also reveals the additional significance or fullness of baptism in the light of the Eucharist. This was, of course, admirably stressed in the primitive form of Christian initiation.

Baptism ratifies the reception of the Word of salvation by introducing the believer to the new life; it is birth into reconciled life, and joins the Christian to the ecclesial body of the Lord. The Eucharist adds its fullness and leaven to this initial reconciliation, so that the ecclesial experience of salvation may, as is needful, be constantly revivified. For, in the strict sense, the table of the Lord is the unique actual (as well as sacramental) form of communication of the community as such, and not only of the individual, with the paschal humanity of the Lord. The ecclesial body to which entry is provided by the new birth in water and the Spirit (Jn. 3. 5) experiences its human mystery in the Lord's Supper by participating in the act of reconciliation. Therefore the reconciliation is no longer merely that of a member of the Church forgiven in the blood of Christ and admitted to the bosom of the Father, and thus called to lead a life in communion with his brothers; it is also the reconciliation, to be re-experienced continually and always progressive in tendency, of the body as such with the Father and in him. For in this reconciliation the local Church celebrates and receives the body and blood of the Passover which, reuniting each Christian to the Father and to his brothers, enables that Church to become—within the world—a "body of reconciliation", a *koinonia* established in a love that is always forgiving.

That is why the baptismal reconciliation itself is oriented to the eucharistic celebration, which is its consummation. But the assertion that the Eucharist is in this way the fulfilment of the dynamism of baptism implies that it is already effective in baptism, in the sense that the end is active in that which tends towards it. When one actuality is wholly oriented to another actuality, the intention of the latter impregnates and conditions the action of the former. It takes effect "primordially" in the very depths of that which is disposed towards it; being, like a call-sign, something in the nature of a trigger for action (because of it, everything is set going), it continually underlies the development of the activity in question, for the one goal is aimed at in every moment of the course. As the sacramental consummation of reconciliation, the Eucharist is already effective in baptism, and dynamically implicit in this initial stage of a mystery which will come to fullness only in that eucharistic consummation. In other words, theologians speak of a kind of objective desire (*votum*), implicit in the very nature of baptism and not only in the believers' intention to be baptized. Aquinas wrote that without the *votum* of the Eucharist there would be no salvation for man, since no one could attain to grace without this aspiration to full eucharistic reconciliation—a form of desire already objectively implied in the structure of baptism and which must pass into the consciousness of the baptized person when mature.[2] The reconciliatory efficacy of baptism depends essentially on the ordination of baptism at the Lord's Supper. The sacramental source and the place of paschal reconciliation are therefore the Eucharist. For reconciliation is not merely a private affair between the believer and the Father, but—at one and the same time—the mystery of man's encounter with his brother, and the mystery of the encounter of the reborn community as such with its God and Father.

Therefore the Eucharist can be conceived as the sacrament of an essentially ecclesial reconciliation. The human experience of the communal meal in which this mystery enjoys sacramental life is in no way incidental. In the very sense of the *zikkaron* of the Last Supper, the Eucharist reveals the nature and the demands of the gift that it bestows only by means of the symbolic texture in which it takes shape. The very experience of eating together, in an atmosphere of celebration, is redolent of a meeting in love, a mutual opening-forth, an advance beyond mere intrinsic individual existence, and therefore (in consideration of what men actually are) a reconciliation: what counts is less the fact of eating than that of eating *together* while sharing the same existential blessing.

Perhaps not enough attention has been paid in this regard to the insistence of the gospel traditions on the rite of the breaking of bread, which constitutes the community of the table in the

[2] *S. Th.* III, 80, 11; III, 79, 1, ad 1; III, 73, 2.

Jewish meal ritual, and on that of the cup which goes from hand to hand as the sign of being joined together in the same destiny.[3] These two actions, which put the meal symbolically into a context of brotherhood, Jesus made the agents of the Eucharist, i.e., of the bestowal of the reconciliation made possible by his death. The sign that Jesus made the matter of his sacrament is not the bread and the wine in their static existence, or even merely their power to sustain life. It is the bread and the cup already involved in a symbolic act of human encounter and unity. In this way, the reconciliation bestowed is signified in all its fullness: communion with God realized here and now in the communion of human brothers. A sign of human brotherhood encloses the mystery of reconciliation. As the cross before, the eucharistic meal now renders the profound tendency of salvation visible within the Church.

It should now be clear why it would be a serious theological error to separate in the Lord's Supper the reference to the *ephapax* of the cross (the sacrificial dimension) and the reference to the fact of eating the bread and drinking the cup together (the sacramental dimension). It would entail destroying the profound unity of the mystery of reconciliation. The remembrance enacted is not restricted to the act of refreshment: it implies an essential dimension of the action of thanksgiving and entreaty, the fruits of which (being the fruits of salvation) extend beyond both the assembly which celebrates it and the *hic et nunc* of the celebration. This major effect establishes the ecclesial office of intercession which has its proper place and constant resource in the Eucharist; it is intimately connected with the universal extension of the Lord's sacrifice made present in the signs of the Church. Nevertheless, the profound effect of the eucharistic event is fully active on the individual believer's life only in his receiving of the bread and the cup. That reception is the realization of the very tendency of the paschal sacrifice which is being commemorated. When the

[3] See L. Bouyer, *L'Eucharistie* (Tournai, 1966), p. 83; J. Jeremias, *The Eucharistic Words of Jesus* (London, 1966), p. 232; H. L. Strack and P. Billerbeck, *Kommentar zum Neuen Testament aus Talmud und Midrash*, vol. III (Munich, 1924), pp. 619–20. I have developed this point in some detail in my article "L'Eucharistie et la fraternité", in *Nouv. Rev. Théol.* (1969), pp. 113–35.

Church celebrates this memorial, it asks the Father for the gift of participation in the salvation for which it blesses him; the Father answers the prayer of the Church by giving it the body and blood of reconciliation. "Do this in remembrance of me" implies the volition already expressed in "take, eat", "drink all of you." Communion with the efficacy of the paschal event is actualized by receiving the signs in which the Event of salvation is *re-presented* and realized *hic et nunc*. This is one, indivisible sacramental mystery.[4]

Therefore the Church participates in the paschal reconciliation (with its two dimensions opening the Church to the Father and to humankind) by means of the sacramental action of sharing in common the bread and the cup which, in their ultimate depth of significance, have become the body and blood of Christ. This action shows forth the effect desired by the Lord. The eucharistic grace must pierce the brotherhood of the table, which is quite precarious (because of the sin which turns every Christian in upon himself), and always limited. Grace enables the Christian to perceive his ideal image in the transient action of the symbolic rite, and to judge himself; cleansing and revivifying him with paschal virtue and power, it projects him towards a culmination which is nothing less than total reconciliation with God and with men, to be sought for again and again because never encountered in its fullness. Therefore the eucharistic meal has an eschatological reference. It is not restricted to a mere celebration of givenness, and to a ritual ornamentation of a fragment of Christian life that is already wholly fraternal—to the celebration of human friendship already intensely manifest. In the actual inadequacy of our ecclesial *koinonia*, spoiled by our enmities (and therefore our various failures in reconciliation), and by the imperfection of our response to God, incapable of reaching perfection in this world, it sets the body of Christ, which heals this condition and shapes it anew so that it may tend wholly towards the God who will be "everything to every one" (1 Cor. 15. 28).

[4] As the theologian Jean Gropper stated in a splendid intervention at Trent (cf. *Concilium Tridentinum*, T. VII, vol. 1 (Freiburg, 1961), p. 406, line 27: "*eucharistia ut sacramentum et ut sacrificium non differt, nisi ratione distinguantur*").

II. Eucharist for the Remission of Sins

In the foregoing I have presented the connection between the eucharistic remembrance and the mystery of reconciliation from the angle of communion, and I have avoided any separation of the positive dimension of entry into the friendship of God and the dimension of the forgiveness of sins within the complex whole of that mystery. In biblical thought, reconciliation is not to be mistaken for the effacement of the past, the forgetting of sins, the extinction of a penalty once incurred. It offers deliverance from enmity and entry into the joy of recovered friendship. The reconciliation of the prodigal son finds its consummation and full significance in the merrymaking of the banquet (Lk. 15. 11–32). For this reason, the old form of public penance had the reconciliation of the penitents take place on Holy Thursday and culminate in the celebration of the Eucharist.

But Jesus' own words require us not to forget that this joyous celebration of salvation at the eucharistic assembly is grounded in the "remission of sins" made possible by the blood of Christ, and that the action of eating the bread and drinking from the cup bestows the fully redemptive power of his death. The reconciliatory function of the Eucharist necessarily implies its efficacious and direct role in the forgiveness and remission of sins.

Elsewhere,[5] I have given a detailed account of the extent to which tradition has always acknowledged this redemptive character of the Eucharist, which is connected to the totality (inseparable from it, according to the Fathers) of the offering of the memorial and the reception of the sacramental signs in which this is accomplished. In taking the bread and the cup of expiation, the believer participates in the propitiatory power of the cross. His sins also are wiped out. The best scholastic thought did not dispense with this way of conceiving the relation of the Eucharist to the *ephapax* of the death of Christ, even though it distinguished "sacrifice" from "sacrament". Aquinas makes the following categorical assertion in regard to communion: "Considered in itself (*secundum se*), this sacrament has the power to remit all sins, and derives this power from the passion of Christ which is the source and cause of the remission of sins".[6]

[5] *L'Eucharistie Pâque de l'Eglise* (Paris, 1964).

[6] *S. Th.* III, 79, 3. See also *In I ad Cor.*, Lect. 6, no. 682.

In the most realistic sense of the term, the Eucharist is the sacrament of forgiveness, because it is the sacramental presence and communication of the act which remits sins: as the remembrance of the expiation of the cross, it applies that expiation to those who celebrate the memorial by putting them in touch, through the bread and the cup of the meal, with the "once and for all" of the paschal event itself, and calls down on the whole world the infinite mercy of God, the Father of Jesus. Within the Church, it is properly speaking the location of redemption.

The declaration of the Council of Trent on the propitiatory value of the Lord's Supper has to be reconsidered in the light of the foregoing. Without adverting to what I have outlined in another essay,[7] it seems necessary to emphasize the realism of the Tridentine position, which is evident in the perspective of the preceding discussions of 1551–2 and 1562. Above all in their interventions of December 1551, when the first revision of the text on the sacrifice was being developed, the theologians offered several important qualifications. The reaction of the Reformers made the Tridentine theologians insist on the unique character of Jesus' sacrifice as an adequate expiation of and satisfaction for all the sins of the world: the eucharistic "sacrifice" does not offer another crucifixion but applies the virtue of the cross.[8] But this application relates to all sins, even the most serious, committed after baptism.[9] Admittedly, opinion on this point was not unanimous—a similar situation obtained among the bishops. However, one has to acknowledge that the draft text proposed on 20 January 1552 is

[7] "Pénitence et Eucharistie", in *La Maison-Dieu*, 50 (1967), pp. 103–31.

[8] See especially *Concilium Tridentinum*, vol. VII, 1 (Freiburg, 1961), for the contributions of J. Laynes (p. 382, line 35); Melchior Cano (p. 389, lines 8–12; p. 390, lines 2–8); François Somnius (p. 396, lines 2–9); J. Ravestein (p. 397, lines 32–41); Martin Olaveus (p. 404, lines 15–20, 25–9); Jean Gropper (p. 406, lines 23–6); Ambroise Stork (Pelagus, p. 411, lines 33–7); Jean Delphius (p. 412, lines 40–6); A. de Cathanis (p. 416, lines 12–13); Jean Antoine Delphinus (p. 427, lines 14–17); Barthelemy Carranza de Miranda (p. 436, lines 24–9).

[9] Careful examination of the documentation offers a number of significant statements on this point, which it would be profitable to study in detail. For example, those of J. Laynes (*ibid.*, p. 382, lines 9–31); Melchior Cano (p. 389, lines 13–19, 29–30); François Somnius (p. 396, lines 12–22); J. Ravestein (p. 397, line 18; p. 398, line 13); Ambroise Stork (p. 411, lines 34–7); Jean Delphius (p. 412, lines 30–1).

an admirable statement, especially in its original form as preserved by Frédéric Nausea, Bishop of Vienna,[10] of both the main line of these discussions and the Council's awareness of the complexity of the question. When, in 1562, the problem recurred in the order of the day (inextricably entwined with controversies as to the sacrificial value of the supper on Holy Thursday), the doctrinal atmosphere was no different. A comparative analysis of the various versions of the text shows that the whole is in fact not perfectly well-knit (probably because the unity of the Eucharist *ut sacramentum* and *ut sacrificium* was not appropriately conceived), but that the ruling idea is the certainty of the power of the Eucharist *as such* to remit *"crimina et peccata etiam ingentia"*.

But how does the Eucharist apply this power? In no mechanical fashion, certainly, for in order to attain to the gift of remission a true heart, an unsullied faith, and above all an *unmistakable* contrition and *unmistakable* penitence are required—for God respects man's freedom.[11] But such is the power of the paschal oblation that, to the man who truly accords with its tendency, God grants the grace of perfect sorrow, which remits crimes and sins however great they are; this remission is made actual in participation in the body and blood of the Lord. The text is not clear. I have shown elsewhere[12] why this is so, and justified my interpretation by reference to the entire conciliar documentation. If my interpretation is correct, one is to a considerable extent referred to the traditional interpretation, which is more flexible than the overly myopic explanations current today.

Of course there has never been any doubt in the Church in regard to conditions of truth of life and of heart required before the eucharistic reconciliation can take effect. Reconciliation is not a divine action effected in violation of human liberty. Even though he always makes the first move, God begins by cultivating man's heart so that a desire for unity with him will eventually blossom there. And, anyway, reconciliation means a mutual desire for reunion in love. When love grows to the desired extent on both sides, reconciliation is effected and ratified. As far as the

[10] This version is referred to in *Concilium Tridentinum*, vol. VII, under C 18 (cf. *ibid*., p. 475, note 2).

[11] *Concilium Tridentinum*, vol. VIII, p. 960; cf. DS, 1743.

[12] See *La Maison-Dieu*, 50 (1967), pp. 107–13.

sinner is concerned, the essential expression of this love is contrition. Through the power of the memorial of the propitiatory sacrifice of the Passover, in the fullness of the communal celebration, God grants the seriously guilty though well-intentioned Christian the grace which allows his contrition to develop and thus permits him *actually* to receive, together with his brothers, the bread and the cup of reconciliation.

Theologians therefore recognize two moments in the indivisible forgiving action of the Eucharist: one is more the moment of opening of the heart (through contrition, God already invites man into the full reception of his love), whereas the other is a moment of consummation in which the new covenant is confirmed. Neither of these moments is external to the Eucharist; neither is without its communal nature: together they make up its ecclesial action of redemptive forgiveness. Through the power of the memorial, God moulds the believer who is well disposed even though culpable of grave sin, and who is taking part in the celebration, in order to make him able *truly* to eat the bread of salvation and *truly* to drink the cup of the covenant. This is evidently much more than a preparatory process of mental purification. It is possible for the two moments to be attained in the same act of sacramental manducation. As is known, this is the Thomist theory: if the insufficiently contrite sinner approaches the Lord's table in quite good faith and reverently, together with the body and blood of the Passover he will receive the charity that inspires his contrition and hence opens him to friendship for God —at the moment when he receives the confirmation of his reconciliation.[13] The Eucharist is a whole in which the various components of the one mystery continually blend and interpenetrate to produce the single indivisible action of grace.

The Eastern tradition is certainly aware of this, as is evident from the inclusion in the anaphora of communal penitential prayers that are virtual petitions for absolution.[14] Just as they ask forgiveness for "involuntary" mistakes, they refer to a certain

[13] See especially *S. Th.*, III, 79, 3, corpus et ad 1; III, 80, 4, ad 5.

[14] This point is examined by L. Ligier, "Pénitence et Eucharistie en Orient: théologie sur une interférence de prières et de rites", in *Or. Christ. Per.* (1963), pp. 5–78; see also A. Raes, "Un rite pénitentiel avant la communion dans les liturgies syriennes", in *L'Orient Syrien* (1965), pp. 107–22.

number of "voluntary", grave sins outside the public confession. This insertion in the Eucharist itself is very significant: the forgiveness which makes the Christian fit to receive the Lord's Supper *truly* is directly produced by the memorial itself; that is, by the Passover, but as commemorated *hic et nunc* by the assembly of the faithful. This is an effect of the Eucharist which is consummated in sacramental contact with the body and blood of redemptive sacrifice given in the meal of brotherhood. This is the basic ecclesial source of all forgiveness in its authentic context of communal reconciliation. The remaining rites serve either to extend or to explain it. In addition, with the introduction of auricular confession the Copts simply drew on these eucharistic penitential formularies in order to construct a private rite, just detaching them from their original setting.

Here the Latin liturgy is less satisfactory in its introductory penitential rite, which is poorly integrated into the whole of the new *Ordo Missae*, where it gives the impression of being a preparation, a preliminary formula, without any indication that the grace requested also derives from the memorial. In this respect the West is noteworthy for its reticence. In the ninth century it allowed only a confession of the ministers at the beginning of the synaxis. Later (no doubt under monastic influence) a general penitential formula was introduced directly before the communion. But this would seem to be no more than a request for mental purification, to allow subsequent reception of the sacrament—hardly conducive to the traditional understanding centring more upon the *truth* of the ensuing action than on the purity required. Nevertheless, in certain instances there appeared between the homily and the offertory an adequate stage of communal prayer, including a general confession, the imposition of a penance, and absolution: a usage that persisted here and there, even after Trent. Of all the Latin customs, this would seem to be the most satisfactory and to conform most appropriately to the Christian understanding of the situation of forgiveness. For the liturgy of the word and the eucharistic liturgy form one whole; the word conveys to each Christian but also to the entire assembly as such the power of conversion deriving from the Passover, and allows them *truly* to enter into the mystery of a reconciliation in which God and man are both involved.

III. Eucharist and Sacramental Penance

This well attested existence of explicit rites of absolution and forgiveness in the main eucharistic liturgy (even though in the present Mass of the Latin rite they serve—alas!—only to open the celebration) leads me to pose a certain question. Understood in the light of the discussions from which they emerged, the Tridentine texts certainly though hesitantly affirm the Eucharist's power of redemptive forgiveness as insisted upon in the rites to which I have just alluded; but these texts insist emphatically on the necessity of reference to the sacrament which for several centuries had been recognized as a sacrament of forgiveness in its own right—sacramental penance. Quite apart from the Tridentine documentation, the entire contemporary discipline of the Church is to be called in witness here. Why, if what I have said is correct, must one hold that "those whose conscience is weighed down with mortal sin must first go to sacramental confession, if they can find a confessor",[15] before they approach the eucharistic table? Does not this improperly diminish the value of full participation in the paschal memorial?

To answer these questions one must distinguish between two categories of sins. According to the medieval tradition of Trent, one would speak of venial sins, wiped out by the Eucharist, and of mortal sins, requiring penance; but these categories are awkward. It would certainly be preferable to have recourse once more to the ideas of Theodore of Mopsuestia, of Ephraem Syrus, and of Augustine, who, writing in the context of an age which was still without our forms of private penance, speak of "major sins" effecting exclusion from the Christian community and demanding public penance, and of sins of weakness (unreflected or involuntary) the matter of which might well be serious *in se* but which do not imply any formal rejection of God, and are therefore effaced by the Eucharist. If one translated this classification into the present-day context, one would distinguish between sins of real malice in which bad will is evident, and sins which are possibly serious in terms of matter but which imply a capitulation of the will (if, indeed, it has occurred at all) apart from the

[15] *Concilium Tridentinum*, vol. VII, 187 (cf. DS, 1661).

"pressure of meditated and relished malice".[16] These distinctions, especially the latter, are illuminating: reception of the Eucharist is enough to efface all sins where no real malice is apparent.

Nevertheless, this does not resolve the problem entirely. I have already said that the Oriental liturgies and the penitential rites inserted into the Latin Eucharist after the homily speak of an absolution covering even sins of malice. And, in an inverse sense, Trent was aware that in order to obtain purification of life through the Eucharist, the Christian must have at least a desire (*votum*) for sacramental penance. Trent also remarks that the efficacy of the Eucharist for immediate absolution does not remove the necessity of sacramental penance.[17]

The answer can be found only in a proper understanding of sacramental penance as arising from the Eucharist, inasmuch as it is an expression of an essential dimension of the Eucharist. The ecclesial sacramental source of forgiveness is the Eucharist, which is the celebration of reconciliation in both its private and communal dimensions. All forgiveness bestowed in the Church derives from and is oriented to the Eucharist. I have already noted that baptism itself properly owes its substantive character to the Eucharist. But the paschal memorial stresses above all the intervention of God, who "reconciles men in Christ". Human undertaking is obviously requisite here—an impulse of friendship which, in the case of a sinner, is coloured by contrition. It is enough that this impulse should exist, and one must acknowledge the justice of Cajetan's assertion that access to the eucharistic table makes obligatory contrition *for* and not confession *of* grave sins. In any case, the eucharistic signs insist above all, in this regard, on the divine action at the Lord's Supper filling to overflowing the brethren whom (if they accept him *in truth*) God's

[16] A. Raes, *loc. cit.*, p. 121; see also L. Ligier, *loc. cit.*, pp. 1–18.

[17] For the discussions of 1551–2, see J. Laynes (*Concilium Tridentinum*, vol. VII, p. 382, lines 32–3); J. Ravestein (p. 398, lines 3–12); Martin Olaveus (p. 404, lines 37–42); A. de Cathania (p. 416, line 23). For those of 1562, see, among the bishops' comments, those of the Patriarch of Venice (vol. VIII, p. 912, line 26). For the preparatory stages, see vol. VII, pp. 480–1; vol. VIII, p. 753; any reference is missing from the draft of 5 Sept. 1562 (p. 910); this is remedied in the definitive text by means of a discreet allusion to "*donum poenitentiae*".

generosity reconciles with him and with one another in the experience of the brotherly meal.

The reconciliation ratified by the Eucharist also implies an important notation of a human action: that of the prodigal son who, with a contrite heart, returns to his father, acknowledges his sin and confesses his suffering to him, and begs him to allow his son once more to enter into friendship with him. The father's love undoubtedly took the initiative, and forgiveness had already been bestowed when the son made his move. But, for the reconciliation to attain to its *full truth*, the son's "attitude" is required; this, even though it does not bring about forgiveness (which can come only from the father), nevertheless expresses the authenticity of the call. This is the action of sacramental penance, which is a sacrament having as its matter the whole of the contrite penitent's actions. It is therefore an expression of the human action included in embryo in the Eucharist, providing it with the full space and development required by the very dynamics of reconciliation. In this sense, sacramental penance extinguishes a tension within the density of the eucharistic experience. If, at the moment when he approaches the bread and the cup of reconciliation, the sinner has not already taken this step before presenting himself at the banquet of friendship (which, in a sacramental perspective in which the laws of grace are one with the rhythms of human psychology, is the usual attitude), he must then have the firm desire (*votum*) and sincere resolution to take it eventually. There can be no true reconciliation without at least this *votum*, which is the manifest expression and guarantee of the existence of authentic contrition, without which no grace of forgiveness can be bestowed upon the man whom God never ceases to consider as his free creature.

In strict theological terms, the presence of this contrition (and of the *votum* guaranteeing it) suffices for the sinner—whatever the gravity of his sin—to be able *in truth* to eat the body and drink the blood of Jesus, and not to his own "damnation" (1 Cor. 11. 27–30). In his own time he will perform the act of sacramental penance which, since the Middle Ages, the Church has officially treated as one, but not the sole or main, step required for the forgiveness of sins. Provided that the *votum* exists, even though he has sinned gravely, the Christian can receive the body of the Lord without previous sacramental confession, and can obtain his reconciliation from that body: one might say that God "anticipates" the confession which will make explicit a reality already essentially present in its eucharistic source. The theologian Ravestein affirmed this in the full assembly of the Council of Trent.[18] Sacramental penance serves only to stress clearly a structural component of the Eucharist within the total mystery of Christian reconciliation.

For reasons of pastoral order which were fully justified at the time of Trent, the present discipline, which relies (if one reads the conciliar texts aright) not on a divine law but on a "custom of the Church", holds that usually (apart from cases of urgent necessity and when a confessor is not available—CIC 856) the Christian guilty of a grave sin must go to confession *before* communion. Surely it would be advantageous in our present situation of rediscovery of the Eucharist and of deep dissatisfaction with the actual forms of sacramental penance (which are felt to be out of tune with the psychology of the present-day Christian) to return to a situation of greater flexibility. Without discarding personal sacramental contact with the Church's minister (but conceiving it as something other than a direct condition of access to communion, and according to a rhythm adapted to individual development), it would be possible, not, certainly, to treat the penitential rite at the beginning of Mass crudely as a general absolution, but at least to see it as an expression of the expiatory power operating in the memorial and applied to those who sincerely regret their sins and are ready to acknowledge them at an opportune moment. This acknowledgment should be made in the exact manner which the Church has the power to lay down, but which is not necessarily tied to the present forms.

This would undoubtedly restore to paschal confession, reconceived in the way I have indicated, its full and proper significance. What is more, the faithful have already sensed this: they have taken the initiative.

[18] *Ibid.*, vol. VII, p. 398, lines 10–13.

Translated by John Griffiths

James F. McCue

Penance as a Separate Sacramental Sign

ANY discussion of penance as a separate sacramental sign must be shaped by two important recent developments within the Catholic community. First, there is a precipitous decline in the frequency of reception of the sacrament of penance. Though the extent of this decline has not been closely measured, it has appeared great enough to cause some concern that within a relatively short period of time the rite of private confession will be but marginal in the life and practice of the Church, and that for many within the Church it will play no role at all. Secondly, there has developed a new sacramental theology that profoundly alters the state of many questions. Before turning to the focal question of this essay—Is a separate sacrament of reconciliation necessary or desirable?—let us first look more closely at these two developments.

I. Decline in the Practice of Confession

There seems to be no serious doubt about the fact that the frequency of confession is declining, and apparently declining rapidly, among Catholics. This decline would seem to be related to a number of other factors, some of which involve more fundamental changes in Catholic life and belief.

First among these is a quite basic transformation of the way in which the Christian faith is being understood. Among many—perhaps especially among the young and among those most moved by the Second Vatican Council—there is emerging a conception of Christianity that involves a much more focal concern with secularity and with secular projects. The Christian's primary responsibility is taken to be the creation of a humane world order, traditional Christian categories and assertions are interpreted in ways most conducive to this end, and the Christian faith is valued to the extent to which it is able to sustain people in the struggle for justice and the good. It is not possible within the framework of this essay to evaluate this movement. However, it is important to note that within this emerging framework the traditional penitential rite seems strangely out of place. The emphasis within this general interpretation of Christianity is on social involvements, socio-political structures and their transformation, on community; and though informed theologians may be able to discern the vestiges of a more communal past in the present rite of confession, that rite is, I would suggest, ordinarily experienced in a highly individualistic, God-and-the-soul, kind of way.

Related to this shift, though not necessarily identical with it, is a turning away from what is judged to have been an overly pharisaical and legalistic past. Private confession seemed to presuppose that sin (one's sinfulness) was a series of discreet acts committed against a fairly well defined legal code. All such acts could be and had to be enumerated before a duly authorized priest, and his absolution (actually Christ's, given through the instrumentality of the priest) obtained. To commit an act classified as a mortal sin (the general classifications being the work of moral theologians) was to cut oneself off from grace, and grace would ordinarily be restored via the sacramental absolution. It may be possible that private confession could flourish in conjunction with a more complex doctrine of sin; but as a matter of fact it has so long and so commonly been associated with this way of looking at things that the practice of confession can hardly escape being affected by a change in the sense and understanding of sin.

Growing numbers of Catholics, I think, are finding it difficult to think of sin basically in these traditional ways. The conviction grows that the most serious dimensions of one's sinfulness can scarcely be articulated for and submitted to the tribunal of private confession. The reaction to old ways can easily be excessive here and lead to a failure to take seriously the possibility of sinful acts, thus ending in a kind of practical antinomianism. But there is something important and positive here as well. As the Catholic community has in the twentieth century moved out from its ghettoized life and has experienced its involvement in and responsibility for the common life of mankind, our sense of sin has become more political and corporate. We have discovered that our lives are entwined in subtle (and at times in not so subtle) and inescapable ways with wrong-doing and viciousness. In the very marrow of our lives we are implicated in national, racial and sexual exploitation and violence that seem at the very least as serious as the traditional catalogue of mortal sins, but which do not lend themselves easily to explicit enumeration, firm purpose of amendment, and the consequent absolution. Indeed, many in the West discover themselves to be heritors of a culture that has been ruthlessly exploitative of non-Western and non-Caucasian peoples, and would be very near despair as to the possibility of keeping this civilization from destroying humankind. The naïvely apolitical scientific optimism of Teilhard de Chardin—reminiscent of the eighteenth century, and perhaps especially of Condorcet, writing of the inevitability of progress while awaiting execution at the hands of the Revolution—requires a world and an experience that are not widely available. For those who have come to think that the principal (not the only) ethical questions of their lives are tied up with the issues of world peace, colonialism and racism, the traditional rite seems beside the point.

Relevant too is the ever more complex view which we take of our innermost selves. Our literature can no longer speak confidently, as it still could through much of the nineteenth century, of men who are rather simply good or evil. We are more impressed than were our fathers with the multi-dimensionality of our simplest actions, and with the impossibility of seeing clearly into our own most hidden recesses. The practice of private confession has generally presupposed that one could rather readily assess one's own actions. Luther's claim that one could not know, and therefore could not confess, all one's mortal sins ("*Exsurge Domine*", proposition 8) seemed strange within the older context. Since by definition a mortal sin was something knowable, the opinion seemed not only heretical, it seemed ignorant and self-contradictory as well. Today, however, Luther's insistence that what is most serious and basic about one's sinfulness goes far beyond what one can simply and clearly put one's finger on seems fairly obvious to many, even to many who have never read Luther.

Our sense of ourselves, of the nature and dimensions of our sinfulness, is thus profoundly altered by growing socio-political and psychological awarenesses. In the older asceticism of the three stages of the interior life, sin was seen as that which was overcome in the first stage and left behind in the second and third. For the advancing Christian, sin was something that belonged principally to his past; for the present, and hopefully for the future as well, it was only a threat, not a reality. But in the newer view which I have been trying to describe, sin is a much more present and pervasive reality.

Nor are changes in the understanding of sin the only ones that bear on the question of private confession. The sacrament of penance as it has existed in modern Catholicism has been significantly dependent upon a particular status being accorded the clergy and in particular the confessor. The confessor has ordinarily functioned as an expert in the divine law who, on the basis of his special training and the authority entrusted to him, would see the penitent through to a correct evaluation to his own situation. The confessor, functioning as prosecutor, defence attorney and judge all at once, played an integral role in the formation of conscience and in the entire shaping of the penitent's repentance. Though it might be possible, and may yet be possible, for private confession to flourish without the confessor playing quite this role, this has in large measure been the role played; and as it becomes more and more difficult for more and more people—priests and laity—to acquiesce in this distribution of roles, private confession becomes more and more difficult. It is an important characteristic of the present cultural situation that the moral or ethical prestige of the past and of tradition is low and seems rapidly to be going even lower. The mere fact that many men have for a long time considered some things to be right and others wrong counts for very little among very many, and the reasons customarily offered in support of traditional convictions seems unpersuasive. It is a commonplace observation that many of the young and even of the not so young are profoundly unimpressed with a traditional morality that has strained out so many gnats and swallowed whole so many camels. Yet this general situation is part of the context within which the Church proclaims and effects the forgiveness of sin. The attitudes of lay people to those whose role has been that of custodians and defenders of the traditional morality is affected by the general cultural attitudes.

In addition, certain specific crises within the Catholic community have compounded the problem, or can perhaps be viewed as the specifically Catholic face of the problem. The crisis over contraception has significantly contributed to the loss of moral authority on the part of the clergy and the hierarchy. I refer here not primarily to *Humanae Vitae* and its aftermath. If anything, the reaction to *Humanae Vitae* restored some small fraction of the moral authority that had been forfeited in the years preceding the "opening up" of the contraception question in the mid-1960's. The unwillingness of moral theologians, ordinary confessors and bishops to think about the issues involved, their willingness to sacrifice a good many people to a tradition which, once it became fashionable, they were quick to denounce or even ridicule, cannot be lightly forgotten. Amid a fairly widespread scepticism *within* the Church regarding the traditional moral theology, with the confessor still often thought of as the embodiment of this tradition, it is small wonder that the practice of confession suffers a decline.

If it is agreed that all these and many other similar issues all come together to bring about a decline in the practice of confession, then it will be readily conceded that no amount of tinkering with the rite can altogether solve the problem. The entire Catholic community is presently groping for and, one hopes, towards new forms of faith, action and community; and until solutions to these larger problems take on more definite shape it is unlikely that the problem of penance can be solved entirely.

II. The New Sacramental Theology

The second principal factor affecting the whole question of penance as a separate sacrament is the development in the 1950's of a new sacramental theology. I refer here to the developments associated principally with the names of Karl Rahner and E. Schillebeeckx. Their work has enabled an entire generation of theologians to conceive of the Church itself and the entire Christian life as sacramental in character, and thus to integrate more satisfactorily the entire life of the Christian with those seven rites singled out as sacraments. The seven sacraments are seen as the ritual embodiments of the one grace of Christ, those ritual acts of the Church that express what is absolutely essential to the nature and function of the Church.

The principal weak point in this theory is that it does not make convincing sense of the "*seven* sacraments, neither more nor less" of the Council of Trent. The Rahner–Schillebeeckx view would seem to fit more comfortably with the pre-Lombardian view of a sacramental spectrum stretching from the then clearly dominical baptism and Eucharist to rites which, though perhaps not of dominical institution were none the less effective signs of the grace of God. One might argue that the seven of Trent were the rites which the Church at that time had developed and found essential to its own integrity; but it is difficult to see why it is the case that the Church could not change in such a way that it would no longer find this sevenfold articulation of its activity the most meaningful and appropriate. Schillebeeckx attempts to safeguard the Tridentine insistence on the seven by insisting that Christ must have indicated the sevenfold direction of the Church's sacramentality.[1] Rahner is more convincing by not requiring that the sevenfold differentiation can be traced back to the life of Jesus, arguing instead that "the Church . . . experiences her own nature by fulfilling it, and, of course, what Christ expressly said about the Church belongs to that 'experience', as its foundation and root. By experiencing it she perceives the different levels of her activities by the extent to which she is implicated in them. And so she can recognize that certain acts flowing from her nature are fundamentally and unconditionally the accomplishment of that nature and so are what we call sacraments. The Church could not know this, and certainly the individual theologian could not, if this nature or essence were only given in an abstract idea and not in its real fulfilment in activity; the Church could not abstractly deduce the sacraments, and especially their sevenfold number, from that idea alone. But possessing and recognizing her essence in its concrete fulfilment, she can understand that such and such definite activities which she has already carried out spontaneously in

[1] E. Schillebeeckx, *Christ the Sacrament of the Encounter with God* (New York, 1963), pp. 115–17.

accordance with what she is . . . are essential to her own nature."[2] But it is extremely difficult to see, and I confess I find Rahner's subsequent argument unconvincing, why this activity of the Church cannot lead subsequent to Trent to the taking up of yet another rite or the laying aside of one already in use. In significantly large areas and over significantly long periods of time, the Church has found it possible to embody the one grace of Christ without there being any rite in actual use for the forgiveness of sin in the life of the ordinary Christian.[3] It is not clear that it would be altogether impossible for the Church to find itself once again in such a situation, and presumably it would still be possible for the Church to be the Church in which forgiveness of sins is proclaimed and effected.

All this is said not as an indirect argument for the abolition of private confession. It is rather to argue that it is not *a priori* necessary that, come what may, the Church must insist that the rite of private confession (or some slight variant thereof) be maintained in the regular practice of all communities. If in these very troubled times the Church finds that its understanding of itself is not well expressed in the rite of private penance, it has the perilous freedom to attempt to seek other forms of expression; and it may well be that it will find that which it has done for perhaps thirteen hundred years by means of private confession it can now better do through another rite or even conceivably through a more penitentially oriented eucharistic rite.

If we suppose this to be the case, then it would seem that the best course for the Church leadership to pursue would be to foster an atmosphere of freedom in which the local communities might seek to discover the most appropriate forms for the celebration of the forgiveness of sin. Certainly the traditional form of confession should continue to be made available to those who are still at home with it, and this should be done without the condescension all too often shown to those who still find strength and grace in what is, after all, our common and only past. It would be tragic if the change in penitential ritual were to follow the pattern established

[2] K. Rahner, *The Church and the Sacraments* (London and New York, 1963), p. 70.

[3] Cf. B. Poschmann, *Penance and the Anointing of the Sick* (London and New York, 1963), p. 84.

by the change in the eucharistic ritual, where the old was simply discarded on a given Sunday by administrative *fiat*. We should be coming to see that liturgy and forms of celebration cannot simply be created by act of will, and that the process of growing a liturgy that will truly be expressive of and to a given community is a delicate and difficult matter. We must not thoughtlessly destroy what can be replaced only slowly. Simone Weil has remarked that, "The loss of the past, whether collective or individual, is the great human tragedy, and we have thrown ours away as a child tears up a rose." The remark is painfully appropriate to our experience of the past decade.

III. Freedom for Experimentation

But though those entrusted with pastoral responsibility must endeavour to keep the traditional rite of penance available as an option within the Church, the crisis of which we have been speaking should encourage a free experimentation with alternatives. "Experimentation" is not, perhaps, an altogether appropriate word; it suggests an excessively self-regarding aestheticism that is for ever taking its own pulse to see which of its various experiments it finds most exciting. It may well be that for the present it will be exceptionally difficult to avoid this danger, and that rather than concentrate on new rites it may be preferable to try to develop a more responsible preaching of sin and reconciliation.

There is developing in many places a practice of communal celebrations of penance. Without pretending to describe all the varieties that this movement has taken, we may note that in many cases the communal penitential rite is an only slightly modified version of the traditional private penance. In many cases, the private enumeration of one's sins to a priest is surrounded by more public acts—preaching before and common absolution after—and would seem to be as clearly sacramental as is the more entirely private rite. It is too early to determine whether or not this form of penance can develop into a stable liturgy of the forgiveness of sins. It is my impression that at least some of the interest in this semi-public rite stems from the conviction that one really *ought* to go to confession periodically and that this rite has at least certain advantages over the other. If this impression is sound, this *faute de mieux* attitude will lead people to participate in this rite only as long as they consider themselves obligated to *some* form of penitential rite. But as larger numbers of Catholics come to view canonical obligations as being of principally historical interest (an attitude which, whatever its causes and whatever its consequences, is growing rapidly), this rite may prove less viable than private confession.

Could communal celebrations which broke more drastically with the traditional private confession be regarded as sacramental? Could, for example, a service which began with a sermon aimed at clarifying the nature of our sinfulness, then proceeded to a common and public confession of sins, and concluded with the absolution of all assembled—could such a service be considered a sacrament? We might put this question in context by first asking whether private confession at a time when it was still only a local practice and differed from the practice in some parts of the Church was a sacrament. Private confession came only gradually to be viewed as one of the Church's sacraments. If one insists too rigidly upon the acceptance of a rite as a sacrament by the Church universal as a *sine qua non* of sacramentality, one makes it virtually impossible for anything to *become* a sacrament. Private confession was able to *become* a sacrament because it was introduced at a time when sacramental vocabulary and theory was fluid. A rite could become established in the life of the Church without immediately being challenged by the question of whether or not it was a sacrament.

The Church-sacrament thinking of Rahner and Schillebeeckx has laid great stress on recognition by the Church as constitutive of sacramentality and would thus seem to suggest a negative answer to the question here under consideration. However, one could derive from this same body of thought the view that strictly speaking there is nothing that happens in a sacrament that cannot take place apart from a sacrament. Consequently, even if one wished to insist that formal recognition by the universal Church is necessary for sacramentality—one could still maintain that in certain circumstances and for some people a rite which had not been formally accepted by the Church as a sacrament could be functionally equivalent to a sacrament.

A related problem, and one that troubles many, is whether or not, in the light of Trent, the Church is obligated in perpetuity to maintain in its actual practice seven distinct sacramental rites, and is therefore obligated to maintain a separate sacrament for the forgiveness of sins. The question, it seems to me, is ordinarily put in much too simple, either-or, terms. A separate sacrament for the forgiveness of sins might continue to exist in and be recognized by the Church, yet it could become as marginal, at least for a time, as the anointing of the sick is for most. That is, it could continue to be recognized as a sacrament but would not necessarily play the central role that it has in the immediate past. It could be viewed as a sacrament, but not as something that is a matter of obligation if one is to continue as a member of the Church in good standing. This could take place at the same time that eucharistic piety and preaching took on a stronger sin-forgiveness orientation. I do not put this forth as a recommendation of the way in which things will go, but merely as a possibility that would pose no special problems relative to the Tridentine canons on the sacraments.

In summary we may note that the present is a time of very basic upset and transformation within the Church. The crisis over penance is but one aspect of the total problem, and would seem to be not the basic issue. It would seem desirable therefore that those who have special pastoral responsibilities should not transform the crisis over penance into a challenge to their authority. Rather, at the same time that they try to lead the Church amid its present travails, and as they try to deepen the Church's understanding of the gravity of sin and the reality of forgiveness, they should try to create within the community a genuine freedom which would enable people either to continue in the traditional pattern, to work responsibly to develop new forms for the sacramentalization of the forgiveness of sin, or even for a time to leave aside a separate sacrament for the forgiveness of sins and to discover in the Eucharist the celebration of God's gracious act of forgiveness and reconciliation.

Franz Nikolasch

The Sacrament of Penance: Learning from the East

THE Roman Catholic Church is engaged in a fundamental reappraisal of the nature and purpose of the sacrament of penance.[1] This is in keeping with Article 72 of the Constitution on the Sacred Liturgy, which called for a revision of the rite and formulas for the sacrament of penance that would give "more luminous expression to both the nature and effect of the sacrament".[2]

The reappraisal must also be seen as part of the upheaval within sacramental theology generally, where renewed efforts are being made to clarify the ecclesiological aspect of these signs of salvation.[3] Particular attention, however, has been focused upon the sacrament of penance from the point of view of the history of dogma, and these have shown that the sacrament has undergone very considerable changes in the course of history.[4] Indeed, its development has been so considerable that if history did not so

[1] Cf. F. J. Heggen, *Gemeinsame Bussfeier und Privatbeichte*, Vienna, 1966. W. Kasper, "Confession outside the Confessional?", in *Concilium* (April 1967), pp. 17–22 (American edn., vol. 24); J. Bommer-Th. Rast, *Beichtprobleme heute—Prinzipien und Anregungen* (Zürich, 1968); K. Rahner, "Forgotten Truths concerning the Sacrament of Penance", in *Theological Investigations*, II (London, 1963), pp. 135–75; A. Winklhofer, *Kirche in den Sakramenten* (Frankfurt, 1968), pp. 153–91.

[2] Quoted from *The Documents of Vatican II* (London, 1965).

[3] Cf. E. Schillebeeckx, *De Sacramentele heilseconomie* (Antwerp-Bilthoven, 1952; *id.*, *Christ the Sacrament* (London, 1963); K. Rahner, *The Church and the Sacraments* (Quaestiones Disputatae, London & New York, 1963). See also the Constitution on the Church, article 11, and the Decree on the Ministry and Life of Priests, article 5.

[4] Cf. in particular the works of B. Poschmann, *Poenitentia secunda* (Bonn, 1940); *Penance and the Anointing of the Sick*, Herder's History of

clearly testify to its extent no theologian, given the findings of the Council of Trent, would have thought it possible.

These studies have shown that it is no longer enough to serve up the familiar arguments, no matter how firmly they rest upon the authority of Trent. Neither would it be sufficient to limit investigation to the Latin tradition, where our present formulas have their origin. A stage has been reached at which we must familiarize ourselves with the tradition of the Church as a whole, and this includes the Eastern Churches. In many respects the Western Church went its own way without consideration for the traditions of the East and this left it so much the poorer;[5] this applies particularly to the liturgy and theology of the sacrament of penance.

To gain a clear view of the range and limits of the renewal of this sacrament, a knowledge of its practice among the Eastern Churches, as well as of their understanding of its nature and effects, is therefore an absolute requirement. If it is found that their understanding differs in many respects from that of the Western Church, we should not for that reason conclude that their position is therefore a less "Catholic" one, for the Eastern Churches can appeal to apostolic tradition with as much right as the Latin Church.

That the validity of the Eastern tradition is recognized despite the extent to which it differs from that of the West is clear from the Vatican decree on the Catholic Churches of the East, for it will be recalled that this decree permitted Catholics to ask for the sacraments of penance, the Eucharist, and the anointing of the sick, "from those non-Catholic ministers whose Churches possess valid sacraments".[6] The extent to which the validity of the administration of the sacrament exists cannot be determined on the basis of Western conceptions, nor according to decisions made by the councils of Florence and Trent. The findings of Vatican II are of particular significance for the sacrament of penance because the understanding of the sacrament among

Dogma series (London & New York, 1965); C. Vogel, *Le pécheur et la pénitence dans l'église médiévale* (Paris, 1968).

[5] Cf. the Decree on Ecumenism, articles 14–18.

[6] Cf. the Decree on the Eastern Catholic Churches, article 27; also the Decree on Ecumenism, article 15.

many of the Eastern Churches differs so considerably from the understanding of it traditional in the West.

I. The Penance Liturgy in the Churches of the East[7]

An important characteristic of the Western Church's understanding of confession is that only the private form of it is known, one that hardly allows for a liturgical presentation, and one that is enacted in wholly individualistic terms. The Eastern Churches, in contrast, have a much richer confessional practice that includes communal as well as private confession. And it can be seen from an examination of the formulas for private confession that they are derived from former community liturgies.

1. *The Liturgy of the Private Confession*

It is not possible to say which form of the communal liturgy gave rise to the present rite of private confession in the Byzantine liturgy. However, the oldest collections of texts connected with the development of private confession do show, through their psalms, prayers, readings, and so on, that a relationship exists with the divine office. This is perhaps not very surprising because in Byzantium the practice of private confession was chiefly a consequence of monastic influence. It is also plain that the rites of private confession carry the impress of those hours that themselves have a confessional character—the morning office that began the day (*Orthros*), and Compline, the prayer that ended the day.[8] Basil the Great stressed the confessional character of the *Orthros* and explained that that was why the penitential Psalm 50 was a part of it: "with its words the prayerful man should express his attitude of penitence".[9] In all the Eastern liturgies this psalm is a part of the *Orthros*, which shows how strongly accentuated

[7] Cf. I. H. Dalmais, "Le sacrement de pénitence chez les Orientaux", in *La Maison Dieu*, 56 (1958), pp. 22–9; L. Ligier, s.j., "Dimension personelle et dimension communautaire de la pénitence en Orient", in *La Maison Dieu*, 90 (1967), pp. 155–88; *id.*, "Le sacrement de pénitence selon la tradition orientale", in *Nouv. Rev. Théol.*, 89 (1967), pp. 940–67.

[8] Cf. L. Ligier, s.j., *La Maison Dieu, loc. cit.*, pp. 164–7.

[9] Basil the Greater, *Letter 207 to the Priests of Neocesarea*. Cf. J. Mateos, s.j., "L'office monastique à la fine du IVe siècle: Antioche, Palestine, Cappadoce", *Or. Chr.*, 47 (1963), pp. 53–88, esp. 84–5.

was the confessional character of this hour. The same can be said of Compline in the Byzantine liturgy. The rule of the monastery of Studion, which states that during the morning office the abbot should proceed to the place where he will hear the monks' confessions,[10] shows how the liturgy of the office gave rise to an independent rite of private confession. But in Saint Euthymios's monastery, confessions were heard during Compline, at the end of the day.[11]

In the course of time these monastic rites gave rise to private confession in that it was offered not only to the monks but to believers from outside the monastery. A similar development took place in the West: private confession of the monks in front of their abbot in Irish and Scottish monasteries led eventually to the Western form of private confession that by the beginning of the Middle Ages had supplanted the communal confession in church.

The situation within the Coptic liturgies was different. Whereas in Byzantium monasteries were situated in the cities, the monks of Egypt went out into the desert where they could live a life of self-denial and striving for perfection far away from the world's distractions. As a consequence, their rites had no influence on the confessional liturgy of the Coptic communities. Instead, this influence was supplied by the Eucharist. Origen had already stressed the importance of the Eucharist for the forgiveness of sins.[12] Thus in the older rituals the confessional rite includes various prayers taken from the eucharistic liturgy,[13] but the connection is hardly apparent in the rite of private confession as practised nowadays, as the priest prays neither the *Our Father* and its embolism nor the succeeding prayer from the preparation for communion, but only the petition for the forgiveness of sins addressed to the Father.[14]

In the case of the West Syriac liturgies, the rite of private confession has no immediate connections with either the office or the

[10] *Constitutiones Studitanae*, 22, *PG*, 99, col. 1712.

[11] Cf. I. Hausherr, s.j., *Direction spirituelle en Orient autrefois* (Rome, 1955), p. 218.

[12] Origen, *De Oratione*, 28, *PG*, 11, cols. 528–9.

[13] H. Denzinger, *Ritus Orientalium* (Würzburg, 1869), I, pp. 436–8; F. E. Brightman–C. E. Hammond, *Liturgies Eastern and Western: Eastern Liturgies* (Oxford, 1896), pp. 181–4.

[14] Cf. L. Ligier, s.j., *La Maison Dieu, loc. cit.*, p. 170.

eucharistic liturgy. The three formulas used today include a liturgy of the Word with readings and prayers taken from the so-called "Incense Rite" (*sedre*). So we can see that in this case also there is a connection with the community liturgy.[15]

The East Syriac liturgy presents a case on its own for its tradition appears to possess no private confession whatsoever.[16] Although Aphraates testifies to the existence in the early Persian Church of a rite of private confession in front of one empowered to forgive sins,[17] there are only very few relevant references in the later Nestorian Church. There is only the "rite of atonement", and this was intended primarily for use in the reconciliation to the community of apostatizers, though it could also be used in connection with other sins.[18] The rule was to petition for the forgiveness of sins within the context of a communal confessional liturgy. Today, the East Syriac liturgy can be observed only among the Nestorians, for the Churches united with Rome (the Malabar Christians, and the Chaldaeans) have accepted the Western form of private confession.[19]

But despite all the differences, the rites of private confession in the various Churches of the East have their origin in a community liturgy, and as a consequence these rites still bear the impress of corporate worship.

2. *Rites for Community Penance Services*

Whereas the Roman liturgy possessed no community form of sacramental confession—unless one considers the Maundy Thursday reconciliation of sinners, a rite that fell into oblivion a long time ago—the East does have such rites. Full sacramental validity was attributed to them and they were often considered to be of greater significance than the rite of private confession.

As has already been noted during our survey of the rites for private confession, these developed from community rites that were closely related to the eucharistic celebration or to the monastic liturgy of the office.[20]

[15] I. H. Dalmais, *loc. cit.*, pp. 23 ff.; H. Denzinger, *op. cit.*, I, pp. 440–8.
[16] Cf. W. De Vries, *Sakramententheologie bei den Nestorianern* (Rome, 1947), pp. 265–80.
[17] Aphraates, *Demonstratio VII.*, *Patr. Syr.*, I, pp. 315 ff.
[18] H. Denzinger, *op. cit.*, I, pp. 467–71. [19] I. H. Dalmais, *loc. cit.*, p. 23.
[20] L. Ligier, S.J., *La Maison Dieu, loc. cit.*, pp. 164–71.

Reference has also already been made to the penitential characteristics of the divine office; the morning prayer and the final evening prayer, *Orthros* and Compline, are penitential in spirit and their daily recurrence serves the purpose of concentrating a man's thoughts upon himself, thereby leading him to recognition of his guilt and of God's greatness.

But in the context of the eucharistic celebration, these confessional rites attain a greater significance. Because, in ecclesial terms, sin and forgiveness involve exclusion from and then reconciliation to the Eucharist,[21] penitential elements belong as of right to the Eucharist either at the beginning or within the eucharistic prayer itself, or else as immediate preparation for communion.

The West Syriac eucharistic liturgy has a general confession of sins and a petition for forgiveness within the eucharistic prayer. Great importance is attached to this general confession. It is the prayer between the bidding prayers and the final doxology, the *"Anes, Aphes, Synchoreson"*, spoken alternately by priest and community.[22] The existence of this prayer is witnessed to as early as the fourth century by the mystagogical catechesis of Jerusalem[23] and by Epiphanius.[24] The Jacob anaphora made the use of this prayer more widespread.[25] In the prayer, the community begs for the forgiveness of all "conscious and unconscious, intentional and unintentional" sins. The style and incidence of this prayer suggest that it has connections with a Judaeo-Christian tradition that can be traced back to the synagogue liturgy. The same prayer also occurs outside the eucharistic celebration within the context of the penitential rites of the divine office.[26]

The East Syriac tradition of the Chaldaeans, the Nestorians and of the Malabar Christians, also possesses a clearly recognizable penitential rite in the eucharistic liturgy occurring immediately before the eucharistic prayer.[27] In the case of the Nestorians,

[21] L. Ligier, s.J., "Pénitence et Eucharistie en Orient. Théologie sur une interférence de prières et de rites", in *Or. Chr. Per.*, 29 (1963), pp. 5–78.
[22] F. E. Brightman, *op. cit.*, p. 96.
[23] *Mystagogische Katechese*, V/9–10, *PG*, 33, col. 1117.
[24] Epiphanius of Salamis, *Haer.*, 75/8, *PG*, 42, col. 513.
[25] L. Ligier, s.J., *Nouv. Rev. Théol., loc. cit.*, p. 963.
[26] Cf. L. Ligier, s.J., *La Maison Dieu, loc. cit.*, p. 176.
[27] L. Ligier, s.J., *Or. Chr. Per., loc. cit.*, pp. 24–32.

this rite is today the only form of confessional liturgy they have. The rite itself is connected with the breaking of the bread which in the East Syriac liturgy precedes the *Our Father*. First comes an incense rite, and then, immediately before the *Our Father*, the community together makes a confession of sin after which the priest closes the sequence with a petition for forgiveness.[28] That this rite of penance occurs at such an important point in the Eucharist will have contributed in part to the fact that the Nestorians have no rite of private confession.

In the Coptic Church the existence of two rites of penance within the eucharistic celebration led to the present situation in which the otherwise well-known rite of private confession is hardly ever used. Their Eucharist begins with a penitential rite. The priest incenses the room while walking all the way across it as the faithful confess their sins amidst the rising smoke to which, like the West Syriacs, they attribute purifying and sin-removing powers. Finally, the priest addresses a petition for forgiveness to God the Son.[29] It was maintained by medieval writers that this rite of incensing reached back into apostolic times.[30] It is now known that this is not the case, as in the time of Origen incense was not used and neither were any comparable powers attributed to it; but Origen does refer to Old Testament texts[31] so it is clear that the rite is of very ancient origin. The second rite of penance follows after the *Our Father* and consists of those prayers that were also used in the rite of private confession.[32]

A final rite of penance practised in all the Eastern Churches is the ceremonial bending of the knee that in the second vespers for Pentecost marks the close of the Easter period.[33] During Easter it was not permitted to bend the knee during prayer because joy at the resurrection temporarily excludes this gesture of penitence. It was therefore appropriate to mark the return of the practice at

[28] F. E. Brightman, *op. cit.*, pp. 288–95.
[29] F. E. Brightman, *op. cit.*, pp. 147–57.
[30] L. Ligier, S.J., *Nouv. Rev. Théol., loc. cit.*, p. 962.
[31] Origen, *In Lev.*, *hom.* IX, 8, *PG*, 12, cols. 519 ff.; *id., In Num.*, hom. IX, *PG*, 12, cols. 629 ff.
[32] F. E. Brightman, *op. cit.*, pp. 181–4.
[33] A. Rücker, "Die feierliche Kniebeugungszeremonie an Pfingsten in den orientalischen Riten", in *Heilige Überlieferung* (Münster, 1938) (pp. 193–211; R. Cabié, *La Pentecôte* (Tournai, 1965), pp. 111–13.

the end of Easter with a suitable ceremony. The consequent rite was also connected with the feast of Pentecost, the day on which the Church celebrates the descent of the Holy Spirit who effects the forgiveness of sins, and who comes in accordance with the Lord's promise (John 20. 22–3); as Origen put it: "The Holy Spirit removes all impurities and forgives all sins".[34] The prayers in this ceremony allude repeatedly to the connection between the sending of the Spirit and the forgiveness of sins. As this rite is known and, with much pomp and circumstance, celebrated in all the Eastern liturgies, we can ascribe to it both ancient origins and particular importance.

II. The Sacramentality of the Communal Rites

In as far as many of the Eastern Churches attribute more importance to these communal rites than they do to the rite of private confession—indeed, the Nestorians allow of a sacrament of penance only in its communal form—the question arises as to whether, and to what extent, one can ascribe real sacramental efficacy to these communal rites, to what extent, in other words, the form of the rite can be declared legitimate and sacramental.[35] I. H. Dalmais has refused them all sacramental significance and therefore concludes that the East Syriac tradition preserved by the Nestorians has no sacrament of penance, and that the Copts make only very rare use of the sacrament.[36] However, we should not be too quick to equate the sacrament of penance with private confession; such an equation may well be in accordance with Western tradition since scholastic times, but it is not what the early Church held and neither does it reflect the belief of the Eastern Churches. But here, too, we must be careful to distinguish between the various rites, for one would not attribute to the daily recurring penitential rites of the divine office the same degree of efficacy as the rarer rites—for instance, the ceremony of the bending of the knee, or the ceremonial forms of penance within the framework of the celebration of the Eucharist.

The standard must be the degree of efficacy attributed to the

[34] Origen, *In Lev.*, hom., II, 2, *PG*, 12, col. 444.
[35] L. Ligier, s.j., *La Maison Dieu, loc. cit.*, pp. 178–86.
[36] I. H. Dalmais, *loc. cit.*, pp. 22 f.

rites by the Churches in which they are performed. And here one would need to distinguish between those Churches in which private confession is customary, and the others in which it occurs hardly at all, if ever. In the latter case one would naturally be rather more inclined to attribute sacramental power to the communal rites. It is clear that those sins such as apostasy, idol worship, murder and adultery, which in the early Church meant exclusion from the community, and could be forgiven only if the penitent underwent a form of public confession, cannot be forgiven by ordinary communal confession. Some such limitation as this must have applied at least for the duration of the official ecclesiastical penance. If it were possible to obtain forgiveness for these most serious sins through participation in a communal confession service, then the discipline of the sacrament of penance would have become redundant. It is interesting to note that in the Coptic liturgy special prayers for the sinners[37] came immediately after the penitential rites that constituted the preparation for communion—proof enough that for them the preceding pleas for reconciliation were not considered effective. On the other hand, the general belief was that through the communal penitential rites those venial and everyday sins could be forgiven for which no particular forms of confession existed.

Where, as in Byzantium, ecclesial confession was not at once replaced by private confession, the communal forms of penance remained, for some while at least, the only form of an ecclesial, penitential liturgy. If, therefore, there was to be a sacramental form of forgiveness available for the most serious sins, then such could emerge only from the existing penitential rites. That goes for the Coptic Church which until the twelfth century knew no private confession and whose hierarchy then reluctantly accepted it.[38] And, *mutatis mutandis*, it would also apply to the West Syriacs, who set so much store by the communal penitential rites; and of course it would certainly apply to the Nestorians who knew no other form of the sacrament. The Chaldaeans and the

[37] Cf. the Abbysinian liturgy, in which ancient elements of the liturgy of Alexandria have been preserved; F. E. Brightman, *op. cit.*, p. 288.

[38] G. Graf, *Ein Reformversuch innerhalb der koptischen Kirche im 12. Jahrhundert* (Paderborn, 1923), pp. 147–80.

Malabar Christians, however, were in a different position in that union with Rome had led them to introduce private confession.[39]

The foregoing has shown that these Churches did not regard private confession as absolutely necessary, and that the Eastern Churches, even in the case of private confession, did not attach any great importance to a full confession. An awareness of this could contribute much to a renewal of the Western confessional liturgy.

III. The Role of Church and Priest in the Sacrament of Penance

Their role is not to judge the sinner but to speak for him and to pray for his forgiveness. For justification of this relationship Asterius of Amasea refers to the words of Christ: "Judge not, so that no one judges you".[40] In this respect, the Eastern Churches are at one with Scripture, which speaks of the role and necessity of intercession for the sinner, for it is through intercession that the sinner receives God's forgiveness (cf. James 5. 16; 1 John 5. 16). Consequently, the Eastern Churches understandably reject the notion of confession as a judicial act—this being the dominant attitude to this sacrament in the West, as is made clear in the formula of absolution.[41] It is true that certain texts, particularly some Egyptian ones, refer to the power that has been granted to the Church,[42] but it is not conceded that actual forgiveness follows from a judicial statement made by the priest. The norm is for the Church to pray to God for the sinner's forgiveness, and God himself then forgives the sins that have been committed.[43] This understanding of the sacrament is in accordance with that of the early Church and was once also prevalent in the West. Rites and texts pertaining to the Maundy Thursday ceremony for the reconciliation of sinners show this clearly, and prayers such as the *Indulgentiam* served as sacramental formulas of absolution until Thomas Aquinas's time. As well as exercising his role of

[39] I. H. Dalmais, *loc. cit.*, p. 23.

[40] Asterius of Amasea, *Homilia XIII: Adhoratio ad Paenitentiam, PG*, 40, col. 360.

[41] L. Ligier, s.j., *Nouv. Rev. Théol., loc. cit.*, p. 945.

[42] Cf. H. Denzinger, *op. cit.*, 1, cols. 437–9.

[43] Cf. H. Denzinger, *op. cit.*, cols. 437–71.

petitioner on the sinner's behalf, the priest is also required to play a role similar to that of a doctor, whose function it is to diagnose and remedy some sickness. Theodoret of Kyros stressed that the priest should act like a doctor.[44] Origen had already said the same when he urged the apostles' successors to accept the role of spiritual doctor and as such to heal people's wounds.[45] And to this day that is how it has remained in the East, thus fully expressing the purpose of the sacrament that Christ gave us to bring us not judgment but salvation.[46]

To do justice to this role, a priest needs to listen constantly for the guidance of the Spirit with whom Christ connected the forgiveness of sins (John 20. 22–23), and who taught the disciples to overcome temptation and to see into the hearts of men. It is understandable, therefore, that in the East the administration of the sacrament is left largely to monks, as their constant striving for perfection leaves them more open to God's Spirit. Even today they are preferred as confessors, as "spiritual directors"; the faithful would turn to them even when, as in earlier times, they were not ordained.[47]

It is hoped that this article has shown how the practice and understanding of the sacrament of penance prevalent in the East can be of valuable service to us in the West in the renewal of our confessional liturgy. Their tradition and experience can help us to climb out of the crisis situation that now threatens the sacrament. We can rediscover from them aspects of the sacrament that have been either ignored or forgotten.

[44] Theodoret of Kyros, *Quaest. in Lev. XIII–XIV, Inter.*, 15, *PG*, 80, col. 320.

[45] Origen, *Homilia I in Ps. 37. 1, PG*, 12, col. 1369.

[46] Cf. L. Ligier, s.j., *Nouv. Rev. Théol., loc. cit.*, p. 946.

[47] Cf. L. Ligier, s.j., *Nouv. Rev. Théol., loc. cit.*, p. 945.

Translated by Mark Hollebone

José Ramos-Regidor

"Reconciliation" in the Primitive Church and its Lessons for Theology and Pastoral Practice Today

THE celebration of the sacrament of penance in a form confined to the confession known as "private", "auricular" or individual, dates from the twelfth and thirteenth centuries. It evolved from the ancient form, known as "public" or "canonical" or unrepeatable (the only form known till the sixth century), through the phase of what was called "tariffed" penance, lasting from the seventh to the twelfth centuries.[1]

This history of changing structure at least demonstrates that the sacrament of penance is a living reality, an essential part of the historical development of the Church, changing and renewing itself while remaining the same sacrament of the conversion and reconciliation of the Christian sinner. The variety of forms it has vested in the past leads one to hope for a new future for this sacrament, one that we cannot foresee exactly now, differing in greater or lesser degree from present practice. It is the Church's mission to create this future according to the requirements of the new socio-cultural and religious situation in which Christians live.

That there is a crisis now is generally recognized, and this fact makes renewal necessary.[2] This will not take the form of restoring

[1] Suffice to mention here: B. Poschmann, *Penance and the Anointing of the Sick* (London and New York, 1963); K. Rahner, *La Penitenza della Chiesa* (Rome, 1964), historical section pp. 237–868; P. F. Palmer, *Sacrament and Forgiveness* (London, 1960); C. Vogel, *Le pécheur et la pénitence dans l'église ancienne* (Paris, 1966).

[2] Cf. J. P. Jossua, D. Duliscouet, B. D. Marliangeas, "Bulletin de théologie: crise et redécouvert du sacrament de pénitence", in *Rev. des Sc. Phil.*

the ancient forms, which arose from conditions that are far from our own, but theological and pastoral renewal of the sacrament must needs take its origins and history into account, not out of simple archaeological curiosity, but in order to discover the basic meaning underlying the different forms of its celebration, and to point out values that have become somewhat obscured by its present form as well as the defects of its various historical forms.

This investigation will help efforts at renewal, and so the aim of these pages is to give a brief account of penitential practice in the early Church (up to the sixth century) and then make some suggestions as to what this practice can mean to theology and pastoral practice today.

I. The Practice of the Early Church

The early Christian community was largely made up of members who had been baptized as adults, often after a lengthy striving for conversion, under the control of the community and the direction of their pastors. In the earliest times these communities were small in numbers. This situation produced its own form of celebrating the conversion and reconciliation of Christian sinners.

The New Testament itself bears traces of the earliest penitential practice.[3] The apostolic community was conscious of the possibility of sin and of forgiveness for its sinning brethren. This consciousness inspired its members to prevent sin by fortifying each other with example, exhortation and prayer. The conversion and reconciliation of Christian sinners was apparently brought about in two different ways: the first was fraternal correction, the prayer of the community and a form of confession of sins to the brethren (cf. Mt. 18. 15–17, 19–20; Gal. 6. 1–2; James 5. 16–20; 1 Jn. 5. 16); the second, in the case of especially grave and public sins, was a more solemn practice in two phases: first the separation and correction of the sinning brother in case he should corrupt the rest of the community and to move him to conversion (cf. 2 Thess. 3. 6–15; 1 Tim. 1. 20, etc.) and subsequent reconciliation and

---

et Théol., 52 (1968), pp. 119–42; B. Carra de Vaux Saint-Cyr, *La confession en contestation* (Paris, 1970).

[3] Cf. J. Murphy-O'Connor, "Péché et communauté dans le N.T.", in *Rev. Bib.*, 74 (1967), pp. 161–93.

reintegration into the social and cultural life of the community once his conversion seemed to be fully assured (cf. 2 Cor. 5. 2–11; it does not seem quite clear whether 1 Timothy 5. 20–2 has a penitential or "ministerial" meaning).

This penitential practice was carried out by the whole community, intimately linked to the special function of its pastors. The texts of Matthew 16. 18–19 and 18. 18 and John 22–3 witness to the fact that the practice was based on the expressed will of Jesus Christ, who communicated the capacity to forgive Christian sinners while imposing certain conditions on them as a sign and guarantee of their conversion[4] to his Church, organized around its pastors (the apostles and their successors).

Later writers who supply evidence of the practice are Clement of Rome, Ignatius of Antioch, and particularly the Shepherd of Hermas and some writings of Ireneaus and Clement of Alexandria. These are fragmentary and occasional texts, and are not always easy to interpret. Later ones, of the third century, especially in Tertullian, Cyprian and Origen, are richer in detail and in doctrine. From the fourth century, texts are far more numerous, and penitential discipline appears to be established in its essentials in norms laid down by Councils in the first half of the century and in some particularly important penitential writings.

1. *Sins subject to Ancient Penance*

Theoretically, the following principle can be said to have applied: all "mortal" sins (referred to variously as *scelera*, *crimina*, *peccata capitalia*, *peccata maiora*, *mortalia*, *graviora*, etc.) had to be subjected to "canonical" penance, so called because it was ruled by the canons of the Councils just referred to. "Venial" sins (*quotidiana*, *levia*, etc.), on the other hand, were forgiven through personal and community prayer, fasting, almsgiving, good works and the like, often under the guidance of a "spiritual" director.

Lists of mortal sins sometimes coincided with those that the New Testament defines as excluding from the Kingdom, from the Body of Christ, from salvation, but later they were frequently

[4] Cf. H. Vorgrimler, "Matt. 16. 18 f. et le sacrement de pénitence", in *L'homme devant Dieu: Mélanges H. de Lubac* (Paris, 1964), 1, pp. 51–61.
[5] Rahner, "La teologia della penitenza in Tertulliano", *op. cit.*, p. 482; cf. *ibid.*, pp. 476–82, 775–80.

more closely defined and expanded. The fact that some lists give certain sins as "mortal" while others list the same ones as "venial" indicates that the distinction, even in the sixth century, was still thoroughly flexible and fluid.

This flexibility, coupled with the fact that (for reasons to be outlined shortly) few Christians had recourse to canonical penance, meant that, despite the continuing theoretical validity of the distinction, "it is open to doubt whether ecclesiastical penance, *in practice*, extended much beyond notorious cases of capital sin".[5]

2. *The Liturgy of Penance*

A penitential liturgy begins to take shape in the texts of the third century. Taking the clarifications of later texts into account, and bearing the peculiarities of each Church in mind, one can say that the penitential liturgy of the early Church was made up of these three elements:

(*a*) *Going in among the penitents.* This consisted of a liturgical rite, known as "*petere paenitentiam*", "*imponere paenitentiam*", "*accipere paenitentiam*", "*exhomolgesi*", etc., made up of various gestures such as the laying on of hands, dressing in sackcloth and symbolic expulsion from the community to enter into the "order" or group of penitents. To put oneself forward to undergo this rite was to acknowledge oneself in public to be a sinner. The rite sometimes required a public, though non-specific, confession of sins. There is a letter from St Leo the Great in which he prohibits detailed public confession, on the grounds that it is sufficient for this detailed confession to have been made privately to the bishop.[6] The bishop could himself take the initiative and even excommunicate public sinners, or exclude them from the Church, if they were not prepared to submit to canonical penance.

(*b*) *"Actio paenitentiae"*. This was the name given to the performance of acts of penance, imposed for varying lengths of time, but generally for several years. The duration was fixed by the bishop, taking into account the gravity of the sins, the penitent's diligence in converting himself from them, and the ordinances of the Councils.

During the period of their penance, penitents were excluded

[6] Cf. St Leo the Great, *Ep.* 168, 2 in *PL* 54, 1210–11.

from the eucharistic communion and usually divided into groups or classes according to the degree of participation in the celebration of the Eucharist permitted to them ("*ordines paenitentium*"). They had to lead a life of mortification, devoted to prayer and almsgiving. They were subject to correction, advice and help from the community. They were not allowed to do military service, hold public office or engage in commercial dealings, become members of the clergy, marry, or even, if married, live conjugally with their spouse. And these prohibitions or "penitential injunctions" generally remained in force after reconciliation had been obtained, for the rest of the penitent's life.

(*c*) *Reconciliation or "absolutio paenitentiae"*. At the end of his period of penance, the Christian sinner who had repented and been converted was reconciled to God and the Church through a liturgical rite which varied in degree of solemnity. Usually, the penitent asked for the prayers of the community and begged the bishop for reconciliation. The bishop sometimes pronounced a homily and then laid his hands on the penitent and said the "priestly prayer" of reconciliation. The rite was normally completed by the admission of the penitents to full participation in the Eucharist through communion.

From the fifth century this rite was generally performed on Maundy Thursday. Presbyters could confer penance and reconciliation only in cases of necessity or imminent danger of death.

3. *Characteristics of Early Penitential Practice*

The principal distinction between early practice and the practices introduced in the sixth and seventh centuries is the fact that it could not be repeated, that it was given *once only in a lifetime*. This principle is affirmed for the first time in the Shepherd of Hermas and retained its full rigidity as long as "canonical" penance remained in operation. If a Christian who had already been reconciled once fell into sin again, he could be admitted into the order of penitents once more, and he was prayed for, but he was never allowed official reconciliation a second time, not even at the moment of death.

This principle, coupled with the gamut of penitential obligations, shows that the chief characteristic of early penance was its extreme severity. "Mortal" sin, particularly if committed after baptism, was seen as a seriously evil fact or attitude affecting the whole personality, and so requiring a painful and prolonged effort of conversion.

Canonical penance was of course something *exceptional*, inasmuch as relatively few Christians had recourse to it, owing to the predominant fluidity in the matter of what constituted "mortal" and "venial" sin, and because, in the first centuries, Christian communities were small and fervent. Even when their numbers increased, Christians did not flock to canonical penance in large numbers, owing to the rigidity of its obligations with their consequent personal and social consequences and because of the fact that it could only be applied once. The stage was reached where some bishops and Councils advised and even laid down that penance should be withheld from the young and from married people,[7] and fidelity to the canons and tradition produced the pastorally indefensible situation in which canonical penance came to be reserved almost entirely to the old, and then, being considered as a preparation for death, was generally only received "*in extremis*".[8] To which must be added the fact that certain classes of Christian, such as clerics and religious, could not be admitted to penance.[9]

4. *"Pax ecclesiae" and "Reconciliatio cum Deo"*

The early Fathers clearly affirm the need for and efficacy of

[7] St Ambrose of Milan recommends: "poenitentia agenda eo tempore quo culpae defervescat luxuriae" (*De paenitentia* 2, 11, 107, in *CSEL* 73, p. 205). Canon 15 of the Council of Agde in 506 declares: "Iuvenibus etiam paenitentia non facile commitenda, propter aetatis fragilitatem" (*CCL* 149, p. 201). And Canon 27 of the Council of Orleans in 538 lays down: "Ut ne quis benedictionem paenitentiae iuvenibus personis credere praesumat; certe coniugatis nisi ex consensu partium et aetate iam plena eam dare non audeat" (*CCL* 148A, p. 124).

[8] Cf. Vogel, *op. cit.*, pp. 41–7.

[9] Pope Siricius wrote in 385: "Illud quoque nos par fuit providere ut sicut paenitentiam agere cuiquam non conceditur clericorum, ita et post paenitudinem ac reconciliationem nulii laico liceat honorem clericatus adipisci" (*Ep. ad Himerium Tarrac.*, 14, in *PL* 56, 561). Cf. also St Leo the Great, *Ep.* 167, 2 (ad Rusticul Narbonnesem, ep.), in *PL* 54, 1203–4; Canons 3 and 22 of the Council of Epaone of 517, in *CCL* 148A, pp. 25, 29–30. On religious, see Ps. Fausto de Riez, *Sermo ad monachos de paenitentia,* in *PL* 58, 875–6.

the *striving for conversion* on the part of the Christian sinner, moved by the Spirit, if he is to be able to obtain forgiveness for his sins. This striving was considered sufficient for the forgiveness of *levia et quotidiana peccata* when allied to personal prayer and the prayers of the community. In the case of truly "mortal" sins, however, those subject to canonical penance, the intervention of the Church, the *pax ecclesiae*, was needed.

How the personal effort of the sinner and the intervention of the Church were combined in obtaining God's forgiveness is not always clear. Strong emphasis is usually placed on the former. Some texts seem to consider the intervention of the Church as a *necessary condition*, rooted in the will of Christ as expressed in such passages as Matthew 16. 18–19 and 18. 18, and, though this was only brought in later, John 20. 22–3. The more usual interpretation, based on these same texts, was that the "*pax ecclesiae*" *grants the forgiveness of sins.*[10] This efficacy is sometimes explained by saying that the *pax ecclesiae* confers the gift of the Spirit, the token of life, on the repentant sinner.[11]

It should be borne in mind that the *whole community* intervenes in the conversion and reconciliation of the sinning brother, through its prayers, example, charity, fraternal correction and active participation in the rite of reconciliation. But within this community activity the personal intervention of the bishop himself was also considered indispensable: the pastor of the community had a special part to play in the actions of the community. On the basis of the gospel texts, it was held to be the bishop's role to direct the whole penitential practice, and it was to the prayer of the bishop and his laying on of hands that the granting of the gift of the Spirit was particularly attributed. In this sense the forgiveness of God reaches the sinning brother through the mediation of the ecclesial community organized according to the will of the Lord.[12]

[10] St Augustine, *De baptismo contra donatistas*, 3, 18, 23: "pax ecclesiae remittit peccata et ab ecclesiae pace alienatio tenet peccata" (*CSEL* 5, pp. 214–5).

[11] Cf. St Cyprian, *Ep.* 55, 13: "Pignus vitae in data pace percipiunt" (*CSEL* 3/2, p. 653); *Ep.* 57, 4: "pace accepta receperit spiritum Patris" (*CSEL* 3/2, p. 653).

[12] Cf. K. Delhaye, *Ecclesis Mater chez les Pères des trois premiers siècles* (Paris, 1964), p. 241; F. Bussini, "L'intervention de l'assemblé des fidèles au

It was always clear that the fusion of the different elements or factors of this penitential practice was the work of the Spirit of Christ. It was the Spirit who moved and directed the penitent in his striving for conversion, the Spirit who moved all the members of the community to support their brother in his penitential effort, the Spirit who was present in the community, and in its pastor in a special way, in such a way that the *pax ecclesiae* reintroduced the penitent to community in the Spirit of Christ and so realized his union and reconciliation with God.[13]

5. *Some Data relevant to the Penitential Practice of the Early Church*

Forgiveness of venial sins could be obtained, amongst other means, by *confession* to a presbyter or "spiritual" person (who might be a layman), who helped the penitent in his striving for conversion by advising him and praying for him. From the fourth or fifth century, especially in the East, it became popular to have recourse to monks, who were still lay, for this sort of confession or "spiritual direction".

In some exceptional cases, such as those of scandal-mongers in the time of St Cyprian, or virgins fallen from grace, official reconciliation was granted *without a previous "actio paenitentiae"*, almost as a reduction of public penitential practice. The same sort of reduction began to be applied in the fourth and fifth centuries in the case of the dying who had spent their last few years in sorrow for their sins, but if they recovered they were then obliged to enter an *ordo paenitentium*.

One important fact that should be stressed is that, particularly after the fourth century, many Christians guilty of "mortal" sin were admitted to eucharistic communion without previously undergoing penance or receiving sacramental reconciliation. This is clear from the case of sinning clerics: they were not admitted to the order of public penance; their penance consisted in being downgraded in rank, and if they repented, they were, after a

moment de la réconciliation des pénitents, d'après les trois 'postulations' d'un archidiacre romain du V–VIe siècle", in *Rev. Sc. Rel.*, 41 (1967), pp. 28–38.

[13] Cf. K. Rahner, *Das Sacrament der Busse als Wiederversohnung mit der Kirche*, Schriften zur Theologie VIII (Einsiedeln–Zürich–Cologne, 1968).

certain space of time, admitted to communion as lay folk, without previous sacramental reconciliation.

Religious and sinners who had already been "converted" were in much the same case, and any Christian who had fallen back into his sins after once having received the *pax ecclesiae*, provided he had given evidence of repentance for a certain time, could receive the Eucharist as a viaticum on the point of death, without having been through sacramental reconciliation. The Fathers in their sermons frequently insist on the need for being in a good disposition to approach the Eucharist worthily, but the increase in the number of Christians, coupled with the continuing severity and once-only character of public penance (which involved exclusion from eucharistic communion), it seems that many Christians came forward and were admitted to communion, even though they were conscious of having committed sins considered as truly mortal, provided they gave some sign or guarantee of repentance. Things reached a point where the majority of them could only receive sacramental reconciliation as a preparation for death or actually *in extremis*. And the bishops themselves and even some Councils began to recommend and even require that communion should be received with a certain frequency.[14]

In this connection it should be observed that the East has certain Coptic and Chaldaean anaphoras that contain penitential rites and formulas of absolution, placed around the Lord's Prayer. In them, from the fourth to the ninth century (and even as late as the eleventh in Egypt), forgiveness for all sins was explicitly asked for and granted. This applied not only to sins committed out of weakness or ignorance, but also to those committed, in the words of the formulas, with knowledge and deliberation and of grave matter, except for the great "crimes" (apostasy, idolatry, murder and adultery), which remained subject to public penance. Basically, these penitential rites were made up of a "general" confession, recited by the community or by the deacon in its name, and a general absolution, in deprecatory form, pronounced by the celebrating bishop.[15]

[14] Cf. J. M. R. Tillard, *L'eucharistie pâque de l'église* (Paris, 1964), pp. 117–54; Vogel, *op. cit.*, p. 47–50.

[15] Cf. L. Ligier, "Pénitence et Eucharistie en Orient. Théologie sur une interférence de prières et de rites", in *Orient. Chr. Periodica.*, 29 (1963),

II. Lessons for Today from Early Practice

The penitential practice of the early Church sprang from small and generally fervent communities. As time went on, the celebration of the mystery of the conversion and reconciliation of the Christian sinner was as it were absorbed into the sphere of law, which gradually increased in strength until its general lines had become established in the fourth century. Then, for several centuries, fidelity to the traditional codified discipline delayed renovation of practice to suit the new situation that was coming into being.

It might seem that this danger of "juridicization", of the "mystery" being drawn to and subsumed in the sphere of legalism, has dogged the whole history of the sacrament of penance—one has only to think of the "juridical" abuses of "tariffed" penance and the excessive emphasis placed on the judicial aspects in the practice of confession since the thirteenth century. But it should also be pointed out that early practice enshrined important *values* in the mystery, which have been somewhat overshadowed by the forms of practice that developed in the thirteenth century. Some of these hold lessons for the renewal of penance today, and I should like to summarize them here.

1. *Confession and Conversion*

Since the twelfth or thirteenth century, the celebration of the sacrament of penance has come to consist solely of an individual "confession" of sins and absolution given by the priest. But it would be a mistake to assume that the essence of this sacrament consists in accusing oneself of one's sins. In the early practice, the penitent confessed, or accused himself of, his sins to the bishop as a prelude to entering the *ordo paenitentium*, but what was essential in the celebration of this sacrament was not the confession but the three stages that followed this, in which the whole community took an active part, as I have described.

This early practice brought out that the essential part is the *striving for conversion* on the part of the Christian approaching the Church to receive God's forgiveness through it. Like the

---

pp. 5–68; A. Raes, "Un rite pénitentiel avant la Communion dans les liturgies syriennes", in *L'Orient syrien*, 10 (1965), pp. 107–22.

metanoia of the Bible, this striving had to embrace the whole person, and was demonstrated externally and ecclesially, in all its seriousness, by what I have referred to as the "*actio paenitentiae*". This means that the confession of sins takes on a Christian meaning in so far as it is the sign and incarnation, in an external and ecclesial dimension, of the sinner's striving for conversion. Detailed self-accusation of sins is only required to the extent that it is a manifestation and realization of this conversion.

At this point it should be stressed that the prime object of sacramental confession is not a form of psychological liberation. Confession for this purpose has existed and exists outside Christianity.[16] It can be useful in spiritual direction, but this sort of liberation can be achieved outside the confines of the sacrament, by recourse to a psychologist or spiritual director. Sacramental confession can also have this effect, to a certain extent, but it is not primarily either a psychological relief mechanism or a means of spiritual direction. Sacramental confession forms part of a *religious event*; it is the incarnation of repentance itself, in the light of faith, in order to meet God through the mediation of the Church. The principle governing its practice must always be that quality is more important than quantity. To avoid routine and superficiality, to make confession an event that leaves its mark on the life of the individual and the community, it needs a certain rhythm, a certain effort and a suitable amount of preparation.

2. *Confession and the Community*

The liturgical-ecclesial dimension of the sacrament is hardly recognizable in the form of private or individual confession. The practice of the early Church, on the other hand, clearly brought out the communitary aspect of sin, and the exercise of the priesthood of the whole community in the celebration of the conversion and reconciliation of the sinner. Furthermore, the *ordo paenitentium* involved a certain state, a way of life, and acted as a social sign of the need for the continuous conversion of the whole community.

This is the dimension that modern communal celebrations of the sacrament of penance are trying to recapture, and which forces

[16] Cf. C. Vogel, *Le pécheur et la pénitence au moyen-âge* (Paris, 1969), pp. 10–11, 223–30, which gathers some non-Christian documents.

one to question some assumptions: Is a complete and detailed confession of mortal sins always necessary? Is the Tridentine definition still valid for this new form of celebration of the sacrament? Early practice, and in particular the witness of the Eastern anaphoras previously discussed, would suggest that the sacrament can possibly be celebrated with a *general and generic* confession, followed by general absolution, provided that really mortal sins are confessed privately later, with a frequency that will vary with the customs and requirements of the Church.

The particular way one recognizes oneself as a sinner, whether by detailed confession to a priest or by the public penance of antiquity, always has a sociological value, conditioned by the socio-cultural situation of the community. In some circumstances, confessing a deviation from a norm basic to the group can have the effect of achieving integration or re-integration on the psychological and social level. In a pluralist world, and one in search of new forms of community life, new forms of confession will have to be found.[17] Could there be some use in reviving, in a new guise, the old practice of confession to lay people?[18]

This community aspect also suggests that it is important to find whether and how the conversion of the community as such can be realized sacramentally. This requires a ceremony to express the recognition and overcoming of the collective sin that can take root in a community, and the conversion and renewal of the Church spoken of in the Dogmatic Constitution on the Church.[19]

3. *Confession and Sacramental Economy*

In the early Church, not all Christians received the sacrament of penance, and those who did could do so only once in their lifetime. Among other things, this practice demonstrates that the Church possessed other means of incarnating and effecting the conversion and reconciliation of the Christian sinner. These means

[17] Cf. R. Lemieux, "Pénitence et communauté', in *Com. Cret.*, 8/45–6 (1969), pp. 265–72.

[18] Cf. K. Kasper, "Confession outside the Confessional?", in *Concilium* (April 1967), pp. 17–22 (American edn., vol. 24).

[19] Vatican II, Dogmatic Constitution on the Church, n. 8c: "the Church ... is at the same time holy and always in need of being purified, and incessantly pursues the path of penance and renewal"; cf. also, Pastoral Constitution on the Church in the Modern World, nn. 43 f.

included communal prayer, fraternal correction, the community penitential liturgy, and above all participation in the Eucharist through communion.

This fact suggests that if the sacrament of penance is to be given its proper value, it has to be placed in the framework of the whole sacramental economy of forgiveness. Another article in this number of *Concilium* deals with the Eucharist as a sacrament of forgiveness and with the relationship that exists between Eucharist and penance.

Another task would be the theological and pastoral delineation of the relationship between the sacrament of penance and those of baptism and anointing of the sick. What place does the sacrament of penance occupy in the whole dynamic of conversion that starts with baptism and ends with its fulfilment in the Christian celebration of death in union with the death of Christ? The early Church confined the sacrament of penance to those guilty of mortal sin, and, to a certain extent, notoriously guilty of such sin, but lived the dimension of conversion, begun with baptism, in other ecclesial forms. The question for us today is to find an ecclesial dimension, in various forms of the sacrament of penance, to express this dynamism of the conversion that stems from baptism. There could be grave pastoral objections to going back to confine the sacrament of penance to those guilty of mortal sin, but a diversity of forms could help the Church to live the dimension of conversion, so essential to the individual Christian and to the Church, more effectively. It could also prove a means to a more authentic celebration of the event that the sacrament of penance should be.

Translated by Paul Burns

Harry McSorley

Luther and Trent on the Faith needed for the Sacrament of Penance

THE sacrament of penance will be an inevitable theme of the continuing dialogue among Christians seeking restoration of the unity of the Church. An integral dimension of this discussion will be, of course, a fresh reflection on the attitude of the Reformers towards this sacrament. As far as Luther's teaching is concerned, we already have an introductory study written in an ecumenical spirit by Laurentius Klein.[1] Klein shows the real value which Luther and the Lutheran Confessions placed on the sacrament of penance, but at the same time he points to the difficulties of reconciling Luther's doctrine on this sacrament with that of the tradition of the pre-Reformation Church. Is penance a sacrament in the full sense? Does Luther adequately understand the role of the minister in this sacrament? Is there any sense in which the minister can "bind" sins? Klein's work is useful, but it requires supplementation and revision, both in its interpretation and critical evaluation of Luther at several crucial points, as well as in its statement of the Roman Catholic position, on which much new light has been shed in the past decade.

A more recent study of Luther by a Roman Catholic author, J. Wicks,[2] has not made use of Klein's work, but has raised a new charge against Luther's teaching on penance. According to Wicks, "the first question of clear and serious dogmatic divergence between Luther and the Catholic tradition arose in 1518. This was

[1] L. Klein, *Evangelisch-lutherische Beichte*, Paderborn, 1961.
[2] J. Wicks, *Man Yearning for Grace*, Washington-Cleveland, 1968.

Luther's new departure in sacramental theology during his work on Hebrews and his explanation and defence of the seventh indulgence thesis. We would take our stand with the astute and conscientious Cardinal Cajetan, who made a careful study of Luther's published works before the Augsburg meeting of October 1518. Cajetan's principal objection was to Luther's idea of the kind of faith required for fruitful reception of the sacrament of penance. ... The critical point over which Cajetan and Luther argued was not ... the necessity of faith for fruitful reception of a sacrament. The issue was, rather, the kind of faith that Luther said was necessary for forgiveness in confession. In the account of his position, written in November 1518, Luther called this [faith in the present effect] *fides de effectu praesenti*."[3]

The purpose of this article is to show that Luther's conception of the kind of faith required for fruitful reception of the sacrament of penance not only is not "a clear and serious dogmatic divergence" from the Catholic tradition, but is a viewpoint that, in essence, was defended by several Catholic bishops at the Council of Trent. This was one of the main reasons why Trent refrained from simply repeating the censure of Luther's thesis about the kind of faith necessary for the reception of penance that had been made in that highly ambiguous papal document of 1520, *Exsurge Domine*.[4]

I. The Medieval Background

Before outlining Luther's position and Trent's reaction to it, three important observations ought to be made concerning the remote and the immediate theological context of Luther's doctrine about the kind of faith required for the effective reception of penance. First, given the enormous diversity of the scholastic theological expositions of the sacrament of penance and the paucity of magisterial decisions, it is antecedently improbable that Luther's view about the kind of faith required for the fruitfulness of the sacrament would be such as to be a "clear and serious

[3] *Ibid.*, p. 13.

[4] Concerning this ambiguity see my study, *Luther: Right or Wrong*, New York–Minneapolis, 1969, pp. 251–3 (*Luthers Lehre vom unfreien Willen*, Munich, 1967).

dogmatic divergence" from the Catholic tradition. Even the Nominalist teaching on penance kept within the bounds of orthodoxy, since "on the disputed points, including the effect of absolution, no decision of the magisterium was available."[5]

Second, without minimizing in any way the talents, astuteness and conscientiousness of Cajetan, it is somewhat risky to take one's stand in evaluating Luther's doctrine with a man whose own theology of the kind of contrition required for the sacrament of penance was itself found wanting at Trent. Although he asserts that Cajetan was "the best interpreter of Thomist and Catholic thought" on the eve of the Council of Trent, A. Michel concedes that, on several points of sacramental theology, it was Cajetan who went in new directions and broke with St Thomas.[6]

Furthermore, to determine that the critical point over which Luther and Cajetan argued at Augsburg, or even that the focus of Cajetan's principal objection was Luther's idea of the kind of faith required for fruitful reception of penance, is still a long way from proving that Luther's position embodied a "clear and serious dogmatic divergence".

Third, to prove that Luther's view was really a clear and serious dogmatic divergence one would have to show (*a*) that despite their disagreement on so many questions pertaining to the sacrament of penance, the medieval scholastics were practically in unanimous agreement that the faith required for fruitful reception of the sacrament could in no way include or be harmonized with Luther's view, or (*b*) that there is either some clear biblical doctrine or some clear conciliar or papal dogma that was clearly contradicted by Luther's teaching.

II. Luther's Position

Wicks is correct in pointing out that the controversy between Cajetan and Luther centred not on the necessity of faith required for fruitful reception of penance, but on the *kind* of faith that Luther said was necessary. In his lectures on the Epistle to the Hebrews (1517) Luther, invoking St Bernard of Clairvaux for

[5] B. Poschmann, *Penance and the Anointing of the Sick*, London and New York, 1964 (*Busse und Letzte Ölung*, Freiburg, 1951), p. 192.

[6] A. Michel, "Pénitence", in *Dict. Théol. Cath.*, 12, pp. 1016–19, 1084.

support, insisted that "no one receives grace because he is absolved ... but because he believes that by being absolved he receives grace."[7] Further it is not enough to believe that God is able to forgive my sins; I must believe in all certainty that my sins are forgiven.[8]

In 1518, in the explanation of the seventh of his ninety-five indulgence theses, Luther teaches that, in approaching the priest for absolution, the penitent, if he is to have true peace of heart, must have a firm faith or belief in the promise of Christ: "Whatever you loose on earth will be loosed in heaven." If the penitent doubts this word, that is, does not believe confidently in it, "even though he be pardoned a million times ... he shall never know inner peace."[9] "As a general rule", continues Luther, "we are not sure of the remission of guilt, except through the judgment of the priest, and not even through him unless you believe in Christ who has promised, 'Whatever you shall loose, etc.'."[10] Roman Catholics, long accustomed in the pre-Vatican II era to being told "God can forgive your sins directly, but you're only *sure* they're forgiven if you go to confession", will find Luther's explanation of the confident certitude we ought to have concerning sacramental absolution quite unrevolutionary.[11] It surely does not strike us as "the beginning of the Reformation and of the oft-sought 'reformation element' in Luther's theology".[12] Is Luther's insistence that, in order to receive the sacrament of penance fruitfully, one must believe with certainty in "the present effect" of the sacrament really not just a "new departure" in sacramental *theology*, but also a clear and serious *dogmatic* divergence?[13]

[7] WA 57/III, 169, 23: *Luther's Works* [=LW], vol. 29, St Louis, 1968, p. 172. [8] WA 57/III, 169, 15. Cf. Wicks, p. 213.

[9] WA I, 541; LW 31, 100 f.

[10] *Ibid.*; LW 31, 101. An author whose position is similar to that of Wicks, P. Hacker, *Das Ich im Glauben bei Martin Luther*, Graz, 1966, p. 80, misses an important distinction here when he attributes to Luther the view that a person only obtains "remission of sins because of his firm belief in the sin being forgiven". Luther explicitly states, in agreement with the scholastics, that remission can take place before we seek absolution from a priest.

[11] No more than his contemporaries or his scholastic predecessors did Luther appreciate the idea that reconciliation with the Church is the immediate effect of the sacrament of penance. Cf. Poschmann, p. 208.

[12] Wicks, p. 257.

[13] WA 2, 14, 25 and 15, 7; LW 31, pp. 273 f. Cf. Wicks, pp. 214 f.

Before turning to the official response of the Church to Luther's teaching, it is important to note, firstly, that Luther was genuinely astonished that Cajetan should attack the concept of faith he had taught in his explanation of the seventh indulgence thesis.[14] He thought it was such an accepted doctrine that no one would ever call it into question. One has to conclude, therefore, that at least on this point Luther was in no way conscious of having broken with the Catholic tradition.

Secondly, Luther regards his teaching concerning the kind of faith required for fruitful reception of a sacrament as traditional because it is supported by a number of New Testament passages as well as by the testimony of St Augustine and St Bernard.

In the *Resolutiones* and the *Acta Augustana* of 1518, as well as in the *Defence and Explanation of All the Articles* of 1521, Luther uses more than a dozen New Testament texts to support his thesis. Although Hacker[15] rightly criticizes Luther's exegesis at some points, his own reading of the texts leaves much to be desired. In any case he does not, as he thinks, "devastate" Luther's biblical argument. The citation from St Bernard[16] is further indication that Luther was not conscious of diverging from the Catholic tradition on this point. Even if Wicks were correct in asserting that Luther's interpretation of Augustine and Bernard is "doubtful" (p. 378), this is still not a demonstration that Luther's interpretation represented a clear and serious *dogmatic* divergence from them and the rest of the tradition.

Thirdly, it must be noted that, rightly or wrongly, Luther understood Cajetan to be saying that "every person going to the sacrament was uncertain whether or not he would receive grace".[17] *If* this were Cajetan's position—and it is not our task to settle this question here—then it is Cajetan, not Luther, who has broken with the tradition of the Church. And it would be Cajetan, not Luther, whose teaching is at odds with the doctrine of Trent.

The best summary of Luther's position can be made by using

[14] WA 2, 7; LW 31, 261 f. Cf. WA 7, 371–6; LW 32, 45 f.

[15] *Op. cit.*

[16] WA 2, 15; LW 31, 274. Bernard was also cited to this same effect in the *Lectures on Hebrews* of 1517: WA 57/III, 169, 23; cf. Wicks, p. 212.

[17] WA 2, 7; LW 31, 261.

his own words: "a person going to the sacrament must believe that he will receive grace, and not doubt it, but have absolute confidence, otherwise he will do so to his own condemnation".[18] Why is Luther so concerned about asserting and defending this thesis? He gives us the answer in his book of 1521, *Defence and Explanation of All the Articles*, where he claims he is simply taking seriously the article of the Creed in which all Christians confess, "I believe in . . . the forgiveness of sins". What sense does it make, asks Luther, if the penitent, hearing the divine verdict of the priest—"I absolve you . . ."—is not supposed to believe this divine verdict? Unless we affirm that we must believe our sins are forgiven when we hear the words of absolution, we are implicitly saying, Luther argues, that the priest, and Christ, on whose promise absolution is based, are liars![19] Nothing more is intended by Luther than this quite traditional understanding of the need for confident faith in the promise of Christ to forgive sins through the sacramental ministry of his priests.

III. Trent's Teaching on Faith and the Sacrament

The bull *Exsurge Domine*, for which Cajetan served as one of the drafters, censured Luther's teaching that: "No one's sins are forgiven unless he believes that they are forgiven when the priest absolves him. Indeed the sin remains unless he believes that it is forgiven. For the forgiveness of sin, or infusion of grace, is not enough, but one must believe that sin is forgiven."[20] We wish to make no further comment on *Exsurge Domine* beyond what we have made above.[21] But what about the Council of Trent? Did it regard Luther's teaching on the kind of faith required for fruitful reception of penance as a clear and serious dogmatic divergence?

When Trent teaches in its sixth chapter on the sacrament of penance that the "penitent ought not . . . think that by his faith alone he is truly absolved in God's sight" Luther's teaching is in no way rebuked.[22] It should be clear from what we have already

[18] WA 2, 13; LW 31, 271.
[19] WA 7, 371–3; LW 32, 43–5.
[20] Denz. 1460.
[21] *Supra*, n. 4.
[22] Session XIV (1551); Denz. 1685.

seen that Luther did not think priestly absolution was unnecessary. One should not draw such a conclusion even in the face of Luther's frequent references to the then familiar dictum: "It is not the sacrament, but faith in the sacrament that justifies." It is the faith of the *sacrament*, not faith alone, in this context at least, that justifies.[23]

Nor is Luther's view rejected when, in part two of canon 6 on penance, the Council refuses to recognize "the faith . . . by which someone believes his sins are forgiven by Christ" as a "part" of the sacrament. "Part" is used here in the scholastic sense to designate the specific elements of a sacrament. The interventions of both theologians and bishops make it clear that such faith was regarded as the foundation and the prerequisite for penance and all the sacraments.[23a]

Trent came to grips with Luther's thesis on the kind of faith required for effective reception of a sacrament not in its doctrine on penance of 1551, but in its teaching on the sacraments in general of 1547. On 17 January 1547, a list of fourteen "errors of the heretics" was proposed to the General Congregation for examination. Article 5 on this list read as follows: "The sacraments never give grace or forgiveness of sins but only the faith in the sacrament."[24] Article 7 was similar: "The sacraments only give grace to those who believe their sins are forgiven."[25] Articles 5 and 7 were eventually merged into what later became, in its final form, canon 8 on the sacraments in general.[26] During discussion of article 5, Cardinal Seripando, invoking St Augustine, made the clarification that, if faith be lacking, baptism is ineffective. "Therefore," he continued, "the forgiveness of sins is attributed not only to faith, but to the sacrament and to faith"—a view perfectly in harmony with Luther's teaching.[26a]

[23] V. Vajta, "De la participation au salut: sacrement et foi", in *Irenikon*, 38 (1965), pp. 153–7, has already pointed this out in his critique of L. Vilette's *Foi et Sacrement* (1959).

[23a] Cf. *Concilium Tridentinum Diariorum* . . . ed. Societas Goerresiana, Freiburg, 1964², tom. 7, 253, 36 f.; 255, 14; 272, 4; 275, 15; 293, 29 f. and esp. 308, 17.

[24] *Conc. Trid*. 5, 836, 5 f. All subsequent references will be from tom. 5 and therefore will be cited simply according to page and line.

[25] 836, 14.

[26] Denz. 1608.

[26a] 962, 10 f.

The seventh article was examined by the theologians, some of whom held it was heretical,[27] or already condemned either in the decree on justification[28] or in *Exsurge Domine*,[29] while others maintained that it was false, but not heretical,[30] that it should not be rejected without qualification,[31] that it should be censured only in the "Lutheran sense",[32] or that it is not heretical at all.[33] This divided state of theological opinion at Trent should be sufficient indication that there was no *clear* dogmatic commitment of the Church on this question prior to Trent.

During the General Congregation at least seven Council Fathers said that the seventh article should not be condemned without some explanation, for it can have a true meaning.[34] Others, including a spokesman for the several Benedictine abbots present, said the article should not be condemned at all.[35] H. Jedin has pointed out that these bishops stressed not only the necessity of faith, but "faith in the sacrament as effecting grace when received".[35a] This view, corresponding fully to Luther's, was not condemned at Trent.

Cardinal Seripando's intervention was significant. He pointed out that the article is subject to two interpretations: (1) Grace is only given through the sacraments to those who believe their sins are forgiven in the sacrament. The article cannot be condemned according to this understanding of it, he argued, because, as Augustine has said: "Those who don't believe their sins are forgiven are not forgiven."[36] (2) Another interpretation of the

[27] 850, 22; 853, 23; 854, 7; 855, 26; 861, 40; 862, 8 f.

[28] 848, 14 f.; 849, 33 f.; 852, 31; 854, 7; 855, 26; 860, 6 f.; 862, 8 f. For Trent's teaching on certitude in relation to justification cf. H. Küng, *Justification*, London and New York, 1964, pp. 254 ff. (*Rechtfertigung*, Einsiedeln, 1957).

[29] 851, 13 and 19.

[30] This would be a theological but not a dogmatic divergence: 849, 47; 852, 15; 860, 31 f.

[31] 846, 16 f.; 856, 35.

[32] 849, 7 f.; 850, 33. No explanation is offered, however, as to what the "Lutheran understanding" is!

[33] 845, 5 ff. and 33 f.

[34] 903, 11; 924, 15 ff.; 927, 25 f. and 35 f.; 931, 11; 933, 4 f. and 24 f. and esp. 971, 6 ff.

[35] 925, 1; 936, 12 ff. and 24 ff.

[35a] H. Jedin, *A History of the Council of Trent*, St Louis, 1961, vol. II, p. 382 (*Geschichte des Konzils von Trient*, Freiburg, 1959).

[36] 962, 13–16; cf. *De doctr. Christ.*, lib. I, cap. 18: *Migne*, 34, 25.

article is that grace is acquired through faith alone, apart from any sacramental activity. This is the sense which ought to be condemned, said Seripando, that, namely, which the heretics uphold: Not the sacrament, but faith in the sacrament justifies.[37] Seripando's analysis is excellent in every respect but one: he attributes to "the heretics" a position which Luther at least does not hold. When Seripando proposed that the article be rewritten: "Grace is in no way given through the sacraments, but only by faith . . .", he was describing a position that cannot justly be attributed to Luther.[38]

Just prior to the penultimate formulation of the canons on the sacraments in general, some Fathers expressed the opinion that article 7 should not be censured without some explanation, "since it is necessary for those receiving the sacraments to believe that their sins are forgiven by means of them, especially in the case of baptism and penance, etc.".[39] This is essentially the same kind of faith Luther was teaching.

In the light of the above suggestion the article was recast: "If anyone says that by the work of the sacraments grace is in no way conferred, but that faith alone in the divine promises is sufficient for obtaining grace, let him be anathema."[40]

The final version of the canon states: "If anyone says that by the sacraments of the new law grace is not conferred *ex opere operato*, but that faith alone in the divine promise is sufficient for obtaining grace, let him be anathema."[41] It should be noted here that the much misunderstood and often maligned phrase *"ex opere operato"* was inserted into the canon at the last moment with virtually no discussion of its meaning. The term was used by the scholastics simply to make it clear that the validity and efficacy of a sacrament depend on God, not on man's works, even though man's faith-response is still required. Today, moreover, many Roman Catholic theologians are coming to recognize in Luther's *Large Catechism* and in other utterances of the Lutheran

[37] 962, 16–19.
[38] 962, 20 f.
[39] 971, 6–8.
[40] 984, 21 f.
[41] 995, 25 f.; Denz. 1685.

Confessions the essential content of the Tridentine doctrine of the *ex opere operato* working of the sacraments.[42]

On the basis of what we have seen of Luther's teaching and from our study of the discussions at Trent and the complicated evolution of article 7 into canon 8 of the sacraments in general, it is clear: (1) that the Council of Trent wished to uphold the efficacy of the sacraments, not apart from, but in connection with confident faith in the promises attached to them; (2) that the rejected position which separated faith from the sacrament was not Luther's teaching; and (3) that several distinguished bishops and theologians at Trent defended—without being censured—basically the same position as Martin Luther on the kind of faith necessary for fruitful reception of the sacrament of penance, namely, the necessity on the part of those receiving the sacrament to believe firmly that their sins are forgiven when they hear the words of absolution.

[42] Cf. *Lutherans and Catholics in Dialogue*, III: *The Eucharist as Sacrifice*, Washington, D.C., 1968, p. 193, n. 23.

Carl Peter

Integral Confession and the Council of Trent

ONE's view of the world as a whole has a notable effect on the way one attempts to thematize various relations holding within it. This is surely the case with the Christian struggling to determine whether and to what extent the will of God is expressed in the exigencies that make themselves felt within the universe of man. The student of history must not forget this in dealing with norms that were formulated at a time when the *Weltanschauung* differed greatly from that of his own day. A clear example is the Council of Trent in the research of the present. Only with a healthy regard for the hermeneutical difficulties involved can one reasonably hope to understand its aspirations for a renewal of the Church in the sixteenth century.

Those who took an active part in its sessions had little awareness of the fact that a scientific revolution was then beginning. In this respect their condition may not have been too different from many Christian leaders on the other side of the Reform. Here, however, the consequences for the Roman Catholic Church will be the object of investigation.

One of the foremost was that nature in and around man was regarded not as the area where he could dominate but rather as something which called for his accommodation. It was understood more in terms of what he was to accept than in a perspective of possible modification according to his own designs. In the depth of his own being and that outside himself, man seemed able to effect relatively little change, with the result that conformity was frequently the sole course open to him. Natures might be altered; but even in the generation-corruption cycle, this amounted to a succession involving a basic similarity between antecedents and their consequences. With such a world view an individual could react to his condition or situation in a number of ways. He might rebel in despair or conduct himself with tranquillity and resignation. He could also strive to devise methods that would give him hope of expanding the operative conditions of his own ingenuity. He might even regard many limitations imposed on him from within and without as providential indications of the degree of freedom he was to exercise and not exceed in the living of his life. Very often this last was the option made by believers whose Faith had disposed them to look for God's will in the state of the institutions around them and not merely in the positive commands and prohibitions found in the law of the Gospel. The dimensions of nature and grace in his universe offered man notable opportunities for achievement but at the same time indicated certain frontiers which he ought not to attempt to cross.

The scientific revolution would show that not a few of those limits could in fact be overcome. As a result they could no longer be convincingly regarded as divinely established unless one wished to admit that sin had ultimately been victorious over them or that God had changed his mind regarding their force. The alternative was to grant that man had been mistaken in reckoning concrete obstacles to his own achievement as the moral *caveat's* of the Author of Nature. This is the position Roman Catholics take most often today when they reflect on the matter at all. But the Fathers at Trent did not guess what was about to happen because of the empirical sciences. They assumed the world expressed divine wishes in many of the disabilitating conditions that so often frustrated man's efforts. To think of humanity's modifying its basic constitution so as to conform with man's own wishes requires a view of the world not then taken seriously by Catholic religious leaders. It is with this in mind that one ought to read the Council of Trent when it speaks of divine law in various contexts.

Penance: A Case in Point

This is clearly illustrated in the 14th session when the subject was the sacrament of penance. In what sense could it be said that the latter was divinely willed for Christians of the sixteenth century? The way a Christian viewed the world as a whole would likely influence him when it came to deciding how integral confession of serious moral guilt was related to God's will for the baptized.

First of all notwithstanding their pessimistic view of man's ability to change his basic physical and psychological situation, the participants in the Council of Trent believed that remarkably broad moral changes were possible. Indeed, they discussed these in many areas of Church life, not the least of which was that of penitential practice. Changes in the latter were imperative because sin had affected the rite that was intended to be conducive to divine forgiveness. This at least man could ameliorate with the aid of God's grace. Indeed he was called to do so in the roles of penitent and confessor.[1] That integral confession precisely as such could be the occasion of serious abuses was something the Fathers at Trent had been aware of as early as the Bologna period though the degree to which this influenced the final conciliar document remains uncertain.[2]

Although stability figured prominently in their world view, God was seen as willing man's efforts to improve notably even the covenantal signs of his forgiving grace. One must not, however, exaggerate. The modifications envisioned were not regarded as adding or removing any element essential to the sacramental rite itself.

Recognition of Earlier Development

One's view of what is possible in the present is affected as well by one's grasp of the past. This was the case with bishops and theologians at the Council of Trent when it came to sacramental confession of sins. They were aware of the fact that the concrete form in which they wished to see the rite renewed did not reach back

[1] *Concilii Tridentini Actorum Partis Quartae Volumen Prius*, Tomus VII (Ed. Soc. Goerresiana: F. Brisgoviae, 1961), 347–52

[2] *Concilii Tridentini Actorum . . . , op. cit.*, Tomus VI, p. 407.

unaltered to the Easter Faith of the Apostles. It had been preceded by others in the early centuries of the Church.[3] This was not an object of discussion in its own right; indeed a substantial identity down through the ages was facilely assumed. Furthermore, a very legitimate question was simply not asked: "If radical changes have been made in the past, are they for that fact viable possibilities if needed or desirable in the future?" What did concern the participants was the form in which Penance was normally celebrated in the West in the sixteenth century; namely, in the manner that had become common after the Decree *Omnis Utriusque* of the 4th Lateran Council.[4] Of the various elements that involved, confession of all mortal sins in species and number is most important in this context.

Whatever the correct interpretation of the Reformers' position may be, private confession and absolution were seen as coming under attack from that source. According to the final Tridentine decree, that form of Penance is not repudiated by God, and the emphasis it lays on man's need to be clear and unambiguous in acknowledging his guilt is not latent Pelagianism. What is more, it is not a purely human disposition of elements involved in Christian conversion. Indeed it is in accord with God's will and required because of Christ's institution of Penance as a religious judgment.[5]

Integral Confession and Divine Law

A man may disagree with this and contend that those who wrote this decree were mistaken. Many Christians think just that. But the *Acts* of the Council make one thing very clear; integral confession was not regarded as a purely ecclesiastical requirement.[6] How the conclusion connecting such confession with God's will was reached is another matter. But the fact remains that integral confession was held to stand in a justifiable line of

[3] The wealth of detail revealed by contemporary historical research was of course out of the question. Cf. A. Eppacher, "Die Generalabsolution", in *Zeitschrift für Katholische Theologie*, 90 (1968), 296–308, 385–421.

[4] *Conciliorum Oecumenicorum Decreta*, Herder, 1962, p. 221.

[5] *Concilii Tridentini Actorum . . . , op. cit.*, Tomus VII, p. 358.

[6] This I have tried to establish at greater length elsewhere; cf. "Auricular Confession and the Council of Trent", in *The Jurist*, 28 (1968), 280–97.

development originating in the biblical injunctions regarding conversion in the life of the Christian.

The religious leaders assembled at Trent were influenced by their notion of the divine will. The latter was expressed in the Sacred Scriptures and institutions arising from them. In particular, the New Testament proclaimed the call of man to pardon and peace in the forgiving word of Jesus; this biblical imperative would doubtlessly remain God's sworn will for ever. A development within the New Testament on this topic, one connected with varying Church order, was simply not considered. Similarly the problem of biblical injunctions that later lost their binding force was not discussed. Nevertheless, a naïve fundamentalism was excluded at least in one way; for what followed necessarily from the Scriptures was likewise held to be an expression of God's will. And finally, whatever was required for man's salvation at a particular period of history was for that very fact the object of divine law, no matter how much ecclesiastical determination of conditions and details its presupposed. This might involve a diocesan geography of the world if bishops were bound to residence as a precondition for preaching the Gospel to their people.[7]

The concrete penitential institution in the Catholic Church was therefore held by Trent to be necessary by divine law. The question is what this meant and how it was understood. Concretely in terms of the private character of confession-absolution and as regards the determination of a season appropriate for the reception of the sacrament, the requirements were recognized as ecclesiastical in origin. But some elements of the rite of forgiveness were regarded as a realization of God's own will for the conversion of the sinful Christian; that is in the sense of being attitudes and actions called for by the nature of the case even if men ignored their urgency. Clear and unambiguous confession of serious sin, this to an authorized representative of the Church, was one of these. Thus specific and numerical distinction of sin

[7] Hubert Jedin, "Der Kampf um die bischöfliche Residenzpflicht, 1562–3 (*Il Concilio di Trento e la Riforma Tridentina*), Herder, 1965, 1–26; Johannes Neumann, "Das Jus Divinum im Kirchenrecht", in *Orienterung*, 31 (1967), 5–8. For the opinion of J. Laynes on the meaning of *Jus Divinum* at Trent, cf. G. Alberigo, *Lo sviluppo della dottrina sui poteri nella chiese universale*, Herder, 1964, 33–7.

was considered important, however contextual and conditioned such a religious value may appear to an age that takes greater note of the relativity of human language.

An objection is obvious at this point. The Tridentine canons regarding the integrity of confession include determinations Church authorities have changed when a sufficiently important religious value required it. Instances are general absolution for those in danger of death, an extension of the former to those in serious spiritual need, and the liturgical experimentation presently under way. Viewed in this perspective, are not the canons in question ecclesiastical norms rather than divine law?

The assumption underlying this approach to integral confession would do violence to the Bible if applied there. For it too never offers God's word pure and simple without any determination by the old or new ecclesial community. For one who holds that despite their time-conditioned character the Scriptures nevertheless judge the Christian's faith (both in the sense of religious experience and as truths believed), something of importance follows in this context. In the Tridentine canons regarding penance there are many elements that arose by way of purely ecclesiastical determination. Still to the extent that these canons mediate (which means more than literally repeating) the gospel message regarding conversion for the believing Christian, they have a claim to be heard by those who will to live under the guidance of God's word revealed in Jesus.

There are serious difficulties occasioned by time-conditioned conciliar formulations. A subsequent age of Christians finds it impossible to accept these without interpretation and evaluation. But the question why certain precedents from the past (e.g., the Bible) are normative and others are not (e.g., the Tridentine requirement of integral confession) will be avoided only at the risk of giving the impression that whim or fancy is operative in the selection.[8] It might be preferable to ignore altogether the question of criteria for selecting among norms for present conduct than to propose one that ought by right to apply to the Bible as

[8] The pastoral consequences of such a conclusion I have attempted to show elsewhere; cf. "Renewal of Penance and the Problem of God", in *Theological Studies*, 30 (1969), 489–97 and *The Jurist*, 28 (1968), 366–70, 520–3.

well but refer it only to the 7th canon of Trent's 14th session. It is precisely this sort of option that must be analysed critically unless the theological enterprise of renewal on a pastoral level is to be characterized by a haphazard approach rejected as unsuitable by Christians who expect more in matters of importance.

The Bible and Trent on Penance: A Question of Nexus

At the Council of Trent, God's revealed word was regarded as normative. The Bible was seen as leading to the concrete penitential institution then current; indeed man could not abolish the latter without damage to Christian Faith itself. The nexus thus acknowledged was held to be logical in nature. And in the world view of those who concerned themselves with this matter, a rational thought process involved an analysis of principles held as certain or inference from the latter. In this case, the connection between the penitential institution and the New Testament was accomplished by exegesis of biblical texts (Melchior Cano), or deduction from them (Ruard Tapper).

Biblical scholars today dispute this reading of the passages in question. Systematic theologians concerned with field theories for the development of dogma have a difficulty as well. Is deduction useful as a paradigm to describe the rational activity that for all the essentially personal and experiential character of Faith is nevertheless involved in the equally human need for its thematic expression and development?

Trent recognized notable differences between the confessional practice it sought to renew and the New Testament teaching regarding the conversion of the sinful Christian. Yet the two were not regarded as related merely in terms of temporal sequence. The Bible was accorded greater precedence than that. The Church itself was apostolic and that involved more than adults calling themselves Christians after the time of the apostolic community. So, too, the Bible was held to be more than temporally prior to the private form of Penance with integral confession of serious sins committed after Baptism. Holy Writ exerted more of an influence than that in both the origin and maintenance of the sacrament in that form. The New Testament was normative in the sense of indicating the necessity of an institution embodying the elements of clear confession, absolution and satisfaction. Their world view inclined the framers of the Tridentine decree to see the justification of their Western form of Penance by having recourse to biblical truth, which in its expression led necessarily to another thematization enunciating a need for an institution like the one they knew.

This particular mode of seeking legitimation is inadequate today. The relation between a concrete institution in the sixteenth (much more the twentieth) century and biblical revelation is not reduced to mere temporal sequence if one denies a strict deductive inference of the former from the latter. As Catholics have learned by sad experience, there is always danger of misunderstanding when biblical texts are made major premises in a syllogistic process. But one who would invalidate the nexus Trent asserted between integral confession at least in some circumstances and the New Testament would have to do more than show that the type asserted does not hold. That was the logical sequence the Tridentine assembly was predisposed to see. A world view that recognizes rational development in an analogical transposition of an affective mode of thought and speech to one that is technical could well see the process of conversion that is described one way in the New Testament presented faithfully but differently in the 14th session of Trent.

The Final Position of the Council

Trent taught that for the forgiveness of serious sins committed after Baptism a confession clearly manifesting the guilt involved is necessary, this to the Church represented in its ordained minister. What is often forgotten is that the necessity in question was seen as conditioned. This was explicitly recalled in the debates over and over. It was something the supposed opponents (Reformers) of the penitential system were only too ready to admit. Basically what the Tridentine decree did was to assert the existence of an exigency in conversion, one the ecclesial community might determine but one it did not give origin to and could not totally remove. To be sure that exigency (e.g., integral confession) existed in certain circumstances and not in all. The world view of the framers of the decree undeniably influenced them. That world was the locus of man's free choice conditioned morally by limits he could react to but not eliminate even if he chose to ignore them. As a result it was important for man to discover the responses expected of him in various types of situations. Thus it was necessary, if the Bible in its one way called for it, to state clearly that confession of all mortal sins to the Church's representative for forgiveness was required by divine law even if not always and without exception.

Trent asserted the obligatory character of such confession and made no effort to determine when circumstances called for it by God's will and when they did not. A world in which clear causal lines were seen as holding between God and creatures made it possible to enunciate those that held in the case of conversion even if not always and everywhere. The terminology was not employed but moral and physical impossibility would excuse from fulfilling those demands. What is more, no effort was made to determine what this means concretely. But to deny that God ever willed such confession for anyone as necessary for forgiveness, that was deemed contrary to the teaching of the New Testament. It was also at odds with a centuries-long practice of the Church, in which the Apostles and those whose ministry the latter had commended mediated ever anew God's word of forgiveness spoken in Jesus. It was a general enough assertion that Trent made as a partial, inadequate, but real articulation of Christian Faith. But if that Faith is the fundamental relation of sinful man to a forgiving and saving God, the lack of specificity in this context is not surprising.

Unasked Questions and the Future of the Sacrament

If by God's will Christian conversion involves a clear confession of guilt, is the institution incarnating this in the sixteenth century the exclusive means of attaining reconciliation now and in the future? This is a question that was not considered by the Council of Trent. In the case of concrete embodiments of God's wishes for man, it was presupposed that accommodation was called for. For the most part, only that was to be changed which human guilt had corrupted. Thus the concrete form of Penance in the West was, in the defect of any other and in the likelihood that the Church would not consider developing another, God's will for Christ's followers save where it was truly impossible for the individual.

That man's historical and social consciousness could evolve to the point that the rite as it existed would be a greater hindrance than help for very many ministers and penitents, this was unimagined at Trent. And the world view prevailing there helps explain why. So, too, does the practical preoccupation of the Council. Theoretical questions were avoided wherever possible as matter for free differences of opinion among Catholic Christians. Hence, the treatment of Penance resulted from a desire to reply concretely to what seemed to be an attack directed at an institution held to be required by Faith.

A more recent view of the world sees man as capable of creating his condition though tragically limited in effecting his desires. He produces situations, religious ones included, because in their anticipation they exert a greater hold on him than that of those he finds ready-made. The value of humble and unambiguous acknowledgment of guilt to the Church must be judged today in this context. The Council of Trent is done no service if it is made to answer the question regarding the situations in which integral confession takes precedence over other values that are to be realized in conversion. If it is pastorally desirable to have a variety of forms of confession and absolution, the Tridentine decree cannot be used as an argument to the contrary. Absolution conferred after a generic confession (as a development of what is now present in the revised Latin liturgy of the Eucharist) may well be a necessary form of the sacrament today and in the future. This cannot be achieved without the leadership of those who are moderators of the penitential discipline, but the Council of Trent must not be cited as an authority for preventing their implementing such a proposal. Whether and when subsequent private confession of serious sin would be required is another question. Again, Trent does not offer an answer. It does suggest, however, that the obligation to make such a confession is not totally relative to the concrete situation of the individual involved. It proposed a set of values called for in the conversion of the sinful Christian. How that of integrity compares with all others that then existed and will exist as a result of man's increased creativity is not antecedently clear. But it seems probable that there are and will continue to be situations in which after such a communal rite, private confession is called for objectively even if other values may be sacrificed as a result.[9] To determine what those situations are is not a task for historical theology. It is, however, a matter for consideration in the vitally important process of renewing the sacrament of penance.

[9] One has no grounds for assuming that such a subsequent confession would have value only in the light of disciplinary considerations and not from the very nature of the conversion-situation. For what seems to be a contrary opinion, cf. C. E. Curran, "The Sacrament of Penance Today", in *Worship*, 44 (1970), 8–9.

PART II
BULLETIN

Jean-Jacques von Allmen

The Forgiveness of Sins as a Sacrament in the Reformed Tradition

IN A short article of this kind, discussion of this subject is bound to be somewhat inadequate. To save time, however, I shall not speak of those reformed bodies of the sixteenth century which came into existence as a protest as much against the Lutheran, Calvinist and Anglican[1] Churches as against the Church of Rome. Neither will I speak of those religious bodies which came into existence in the eighteenth century, in the second phase of the Reformation. The purpose of this article is not to give a detailed historical survey, for these are already plentiful; rather it is to point to certain factors which I believe throw some light on the discussion in the Church today.

Luther and Calvin

We could summarize the criticism that Luther levelled at the sacrament of confession as it was practised in his days in this way: he held that to make confession obligatory on the faithful was needlessly oppressive and that to insist on confession as an Easter obligation was quite unjustified. Further, he maintained that the rigorous examination of conscience in order to tabulate sins was a barrier to the real exercise of the Christian conscience. The

[1] On the subject of Anglicanism, it should be noted that the 25th article of the *39 Articles* insists that penance is not "one of the two sacraments ordained by Christ or the Gospel" because it bears no resemblance to anything of divine origin. Sacramental confession was given a new impetus in the Church of England by the Tractarian movement of the nineteenth century, though it never became compulsory.

practice of making the administration of the sacrament of penance the prerogative of the priest was also abhorrent to him, for he insisted that it deprived the laity of an important function in the Church. For Luther the purpose of the sacrament of penance was the absolution of sins, and this for the reason that Christ died to save sinners.[2] It is important to note that Luther did not try to remove penance from the list of sacraments, nor did he maintain that the practice had no foundation in Scripture; it is true, however, that he said that the sacrament was not of dominical origin.[3] Luther believed in penance as a sacrament, of this there is no doubt. His interest was not to abolish it but rather to reform it.

Luther wrote once, "I owe so much to confession, had this sacrament not existed the devil would have won me over long ago".[4] He took its reform very seriously: this is clear from the *Short Exhortation for Confession* which he included as part of his *Catechism*.[5] In the *Shorter Catechism* penance is placed between the sacrament of baptism and the Eucharist, and it is interesting that the instructions he laid down on this matter were observed in the Lutheran Church right up till the end of the eighteenth century.[6] It is therefore wrong to maintain that the Lutheran Church has never had any interest in confession as a sacrament.

It is a different story when we turn to the other Churches of the reformed tradition. They have always been unflinching in their opposition to a sacramental approach to confession. Not only did they maintain that its origin was quite recent, they insisted that in this the Church had perverted the true nature of confession. Above all they saw it as an impediment to the true nature and practice of the forgiveness of sins, so central to the Christian Gospel. "We believe that true confession is made to God alone, either by the sinner directly to his maker or openly

[2] Cf. Rietschel-Graff, *Lehrbuch der Liturgik*, Göttingen, 1951, pp. 805 f.

[3] For example, see his writing in *Von der Beichte*, Weimar Edition, VIII, p. 49.

[4] Erlanger Ausgabe, 28, 249.

[5] Cf. *Die Bekenntnisschriften der evangelisch-lutherischen Kirche*, Göttingen, 1930. This has been translated into French by Max Thurian of Taizé.

[6] Cf. E. Roth, *Die Privatbeichte und Schlüsselgewalt in der Theologie der Reformatoren*, Gütersloh, 1952. Also W. Uhsadel, *Evangelische Beichte in Vergangenheit und Gegenwert*, Gütersloh, 1961.

in the congregation as a form of 'general' confession. In order to receive the remission of his sins, it is certainly not necessary that a man should confess to a priest by mumbling into his ear and should pretend to receive absolution by the laying on of hands! In Scripture there is no authority for such a practice."[7] They were concerned to try to define what the confession of sins actually meant for a Christian. For Calvin there were four distinct approaches:[8] confession to God directly—in private like the tax collector in the gospel parable. This has a validity quite independent of any argument about "the power of the keys".[9] Second, there is confession as practised in the Early Church. This was a form of "general" confession and was of particular interest to Calvin, who studied carefully how it was practised in those days. The sinner whose conduct had caused scandal to the community confessed his sins to the congregation, implored pardon from God and on receiving absolution was once more admitted to the full communion of the Church.

Next, there was the use of a penitential liturgy recited as part of Sunday worship, but it is clear that the reformers who recommended this were basing their recommendation very largely on conjecture.[10] Finally, there was private confession, also known as aural confession. Although as a *compulsory* practice this was abandoned once and for all, it is untrue to say that the practice was totally abolished. Calvin said: "Absolution given to the individual may be no less valid or effective than a general absolution to the whole congregation, in circumstances where the individual feels private confirmation of his forgiveness. There are times when the Christian, in spite of the promises of God, and in spite of confessing his sins in the congregation, feels the need of private confirmation of the forgiveness of his sins. Under these circumstances, the sinner may go to his pastor, confess his sins in private, and be reassured that his sins are forgiven. In this way he will experience quietness of conscience."[11] In the *Second Helvetic Confession* it is stated that "there is no harm in private consolation and exhortation if a sinner still suffers from the

[7] *The Second Helvetic Confession*. Original text in *Creeds of Christendom* by P. Schaff.

[8] Cf. *The Institutes* III. 4, 9, 10–13.

[9] *Ibid.*, III. 4, 14.

[10] Cf. *I Clement* 60, 1; *Didache* 10. 5; 14. 1.

[11] *The Institutes*, III. 4, 14.

burden of his sin. If this is the case he may go to his pastor or to one of his brethren."[12]

THE VARIOUS FORMS OF CONFESSION

With this in mind, we should remember three main facts: the equal validity of the various forms of confession; proclaiming the Word of God is a form of exercising the power of the "keys of the kingdom", and that in hearing a man confess his sins the pastor is exercising his Christian ministry. Now, in the Calvinist Churches, all four forms of confession outlined above are valid, yet this is the subject of considerable debate in these Churches today.[13] Some, like H. Asmussen, would maintain that general or public confession allows sin to be brushed aside and not really *confessed*. In this way the Christian does not learn how to overcome his sin.[14] H. J. Thilo has described this kind of confession as a kind of spiritual narcosis and not a real therapy.[15] A. D. Müller has suggested that this form of confession has meant a loss of the feeling of the Christian exposing himself to the mystery of grace. He suggests that a revival of the practice of aural confession may restore this sense and may bring back to Christians a more real way of unburdening their consciences.[16] In fact both Lutherans and the other reformed bodies would seem to admit now that the power of the forgiveness of sins cannot be "diluted" by being granted in private or in public.

THE SACRAMENTAL NATURE OF PROCLAIMING THE WORD OF GOD[17]

It is perhaps easier to follow this, if one remembers the sacramental quality the reformers attributed to proclaiming the Word of God. The power of the keys, in the words of the *Heidel-*

[12] *Op. cit.*, 82.

[13] On this same problem see F. J. Heggen, *Gemeinsame Bussfeier und Privatbeichte*, Vienna, Freiburg, Basle, 1966.

[14] *Die Seelsorge*, Munich, 1935, p. 222 *et seq*. See also W. Trillhaas, *Der Dienst der Kirche am Menschen*, Munich, 1950, p. 106.

[15] *Der Ungespaltene Mensch, ein Stück Pastoralpsychologie*, Göttingen, 1957, p. 87.

[16] *Grundriss der praktischen Theologie*, Gütersloh, 1950, p. 332. See also E. Thurneysen, *Die Lehre von der Seelsorge*, Zürich, 1946, 263–93 and *Seelsorge im Vollzug*, Zürich, 1968, pp. 178 and 208.

[17] See the fine work of P. Brunner, "Absolution ist eine Verdichtung des Evangeliums als Wort", in *Zur Lehre vom Gottesdienst der in Names Jesus versammelten Gemeinde* (Leiturgia I), Kassel, 1954, p. 199.

berg Catechism (1563) in article 83, "is exercised by preaching the Gospel and by exercising Church discipline. By these two means the Kingdom of Heaven is opened to all believers, and closed to those who refuse to hear the Word of God."[18] *The Confession of Augsburg*, in article 28, states: "We preach that, according to Scripture, the power of the keys is the power and authority given by God to preach the Gospel, to forgive (or not to forgive) sins and to administer the sacraments".[19] So it is clear that in this sense whether confession and absolution have a sacramental character is crucial. We know that Luther and his followers[20] were non-committal but the other reformed bodies decided once and for all that penance should not be considered sacramental, at least not in the sense that they considered Baptism and the Lord's Supper as such. They did, however, place it in the loose category of "things ordained by God"[21] and therefore part of the life of the Church. We should distinguish between the proclamation of the Gospel itself and the *forms* in which it is proclaimed. These would include, the exhortation to believe, the edification of the Christian assembly, catechesis, blessing the faithful, pardoning the sinner who truly repents, the cure of souls, what is termed *mutua consolatio* or the mutual encouragement of the faithful in the love of God and in their baptismal faith. Whatever form the proclamation may take, it is still communicating the Gospel, which is the source of life. It is possible to identify some forms of proclaiming the Gospel which are more important than others (for example, preaching the Word and absolving sins) but this fact can never diminish the saving power of the Word at whatever level it is proclaimed.[22] This would be parallel to the way in which we talk of the Scriptures bearing witness on every page to the fact that the Word of God is incarnate in Jesus Christ. What those of us in the reformed tradition fear is the attempt to sacramentalize confession, because it is our belief that the sacramental aspect of this practice includes also two other forms of proclaiming the Word, namely, the mutual exhortation of the faithful and, above all, preaching the Word of God.

[18] Neuchâtel, 1963, p. 81.
[19] *Confessio Augustana Triglotta*, Strasbourg, 1949, p. 172.
[20] Cf., for example, W. Uhsadel, *op. cit.*, pp. 22 *et seq.*
[21] *The Second Helvetic Confession*, p. 112.
[22] See L. Scheffczyk, *Von der Heilsmacht des Wortes*, Munich, 1966.

Confession and Ministry

In the sixteenth century there was a reaction against the Western tradition of reserving the ministry of confession and absolution for the priesthood alone. It was clear to the reformers that this had by no means always been the practice of the Church. Even in the Gospel, where the public proclamation of the Gospel was entrusted to the apostles (and implicitly to the Christian ministry[23]), it was the faithful as a whole who were charged with the work of salvation. This was why the reformers were so sensitive to what they considered an abuse of this principle, and why they believed with such conviction that to receive the assurance of the forgiveness of his sins, the Christian could turn to any of his baptized brethren in Christ, in the knowledge that in Christ God had conquered sin for once and for all. Bonhoeffer emphasized this when he wrote, "Every Christian may be his brother's confessor".[24] Of course this is based on a much broader understanding of the term "confession" than the traditional sense had allowed, but it did safeguard the possibility of a charismatic element which the more clerical tradition of the West could have been said to have stifled. However, as a general rule the actual granting of absolution or the act of readmitting the sinner to the full communion of the Church remained the prerogative of the pastor in reformed practice. Luther, in his *Short Catechism*, insisted that the confessor be addressed as "reverend master"[25] and, as we have seen, the *Second Helvetic Confession* exhorted the penitent to turn in the first place to a pastor of the Church.

This was also insisted on by Calvin in a passage which is worth quoting at length: "Whereas the Scriptures do not designate any one person to whom we should unburden our hearts, the Church puts the pastor in a position of authority and it is to him that we should turn first, especially as God has ordained him to instruct the faithful in how to overcome sin, to confirm them in his grace

[23] On the idea of apostolic succession in the ministry see my book, *Le Saint Ministère selon la convicition et le volonté des Réformés du XVI siècle*. Neuchâtel, 1968, pp. 23 *et seq*. and pp. 192–212.

[24] *De la vie communautaire*, Neuchâtel, 1947. (*Gemeinsames Leben*, Munich, p. 193.)

[25] "*Wirdiger, lieber Herr*". In the Latin text "*Venerabilis Domine*". He is addressed in the formal second person plural while the penitent is addressed in the second person singular.

and to comfort them . . . moreover the Christian ministry is itself a pledge and witness of Christ's conquest of sin."[26] In all the Reformed Churches it is insisted on that the pastor alone may proclaim the absolution.[27]

The Practice of Private or Aural Confession

After the sixteenth century the popularity of private confession varied quite noticeably. Almost immediately after the Reformation period, the practice fell out of use but then it revived again in the Tractarian movement in the Church of England of the nineteenth century. More recently interest was revived in this practice by the *Berneuchen* movement in the Lutheran Church and also in the wide range of religious milieux which have been influenced by the spirituality of Taizé. However at the present time, there seems, if anything, to be a movement away from the practice of private confession, and I think that this is attributable to a number of reasons. First there is the fact that the relationship of the apostolate, the ministry and the community has never really been worked out, and this is especially true of the Lutheran Church.[28] Next, I would suggest that the fact that Protestants and Catholics have lived side by side for so long has meant that Protestants have wanted to emphasize what is peculiarly Protestant in their tradition: their concern has been to revive the practice of the Early Church by reinstating public or general confession and on the whole they have included this in their eucharistic celebration. But above all private confession has fallen out of use quite simply because it has never been obligatory in the Reformed Churches. If there are a variety of ways of confessing sins, it is only too natural that the most humiliating way should be avoided.

I think that there are psychological reasons for this rise and fall in the popularity of private confession.

The new sense of the "otherness" of the Church from the world has resulted in a deeper awareness of the intrinsic holiness

[26] *The Institutes*, III. 4, 12.

[27] For the formulas for pronouncing absolution see my own *Le Saint Ministère*, 94, 161, and also in J. Beckmann, *Quellen zur Geschichte des christlichen Gottesdienstes*, Gütersloh, 1956, p. 150.

[28] Cf. W. Uhsadel, *op. cit.*, p. 24 *et seq.*; Rietschel-Graff, *op. cit.*, p. 808.

and sanctity of the Church as opposed to the sinfulness of man. I would also mention the feeling among Christian psychotherapists that the Churches ought to restore a means of providing peace and pardon to modern man which their own science cannot provide.[29] Finally, I would point to the anxiety of the Protestant Churches that many of the converts to Rome have "gone over" because they feel a great need to confess their sins and receive forgiveness in this way. But this anxiety has become less acute recently, for Roman Catholic theologians are themselves rethinking the meaning of confession and, if anything, they are investigating a revival of communal or public confession. Even more fundamentally, these theologians are rethinking the nature of sin and Christian morality in general.

We could sum up by saying that the hesitation of Protestants to revive private or aural confession results from two main things: the conviction that absolution is not tied to the sacrament of penance alone and also their belief that the whole body of the faithful have a role to play in bringing the pardon of God to man. If the Roman Catholic Church of today were to share these concerns we could move together towards a new understanding of the problem.

In conclusion, I would like to suggest four main headings under which we could work, for it seems to me that these are the pointers to a solution:

(a) How far may we "canonize" the practice of the Church at a particular stage in its history?

(b) What is the relationship of doctrinal definition to the sacramental life of the Church?

(c) What is the relationship of confession as a community (as a church) to the belief in the holiness of the Church?

(d) In theological, pastoral and historical terms what is the relationship of the forgiveness of sin at baptism and the forgiveness of sin at the Eucharist?

[29] Cf. W. Uhsadel, *Evangelische Seelsorge*, Heidelberg, 1966, 177 *et seq.*

Translated by Robin Baird-Smith

Felix Funke

Survey of Published Writings on Confession over the Past Ten Years

AT THE congress summoned in the year 1965 at Assisi for the study of Sin, Penance and Confession, Z. Alszeghy referred to two important points to be noted for the future: (1) We should not speak of *sins* in the plural, but of *sin* in the singular, since sin is a turning away from God in the innermost being of man. And (2) We must therefore look on Christian penance as a taking back of the sinner into the Church filled with the love of the Holy Spirit.[1] In contemporary writings on the sacrament of penance, these two points are given priority of place.

I. The Personal Dimension of Sin

The first point will be discussed only briefly here, in an endeavour to pave the way for some of the theological ideas that follow on the place of confession in the structure of the Church. Modern psychology and anthropology have made it possible for theologians to free themselves from a magical idea of the sacraments and, with the support of present-day exegesis, to reach a conceptual understanding of sin and repentance that corresponds to biblical teaching. H. Reiners has analysed and evaluated the efforts in this direction in a comprehensive work. Thus—every human being sooner or later makes in his heart, the personal and spiritual centre of his being, the fundamental decision (*optio fundamentalis*) for or against God. This decision thereupon

[1] Z. Alszeghy, "La confessione nella pietà cristiana", in *Credo nella remissione dei peccati*, Assisi, 1966, pp. 77–90, esp. pp. 88–90.

informs all his future actions. It is of such depth that it takes over the whole of the man and, in the ordinary way, changes him permanently for good or ill. It remains true, all the same, given the sequential character of earthly existence, that further change is still possible. Serious sin is a fundamental decision against God, repentance is the reverse. Both are matters of the heart. The moral life of man—and this includes his sacramental life—is ultimately judged in the light of his permanent intention.[2] We must keep this in mind when considering the question of Penance.

II. The Ecclesial Dimension of Penance

1. *Penance as the taking back of the sinner into the Church*

In B. Xiberta's thesis of 1922 he showed that sin and repentance had an ecclesial aspect, and that the immediate effect of the Sacrament of Penance was to reconcile the sinner with the Church.[3] In 1959 C. Dumont cited distinguished theologians like P. de la Taille, B. Poschmann, H. de Lubac, M. Schmaus and K. Rahner as defenders of this thesis. He summarized their conclusions with scholastic lucidity. Thus: Sacramental absolution has as its unique and immediate consequence the sinner's reconciliation with the Church. It is at the same time an effective sign of God's forgiveness, the *"res et sacramentum"* of the Sacrament of Penance.[4] This theological conclusion becomes fully comprehensible only in the light of the writings on ecclesiology that appeared at the same time and defined the Church as the archetypal sacrament realizing itself in the seven sacraments of healing. Thus the Church's function as intermediary takes concrete form as an in-between stage which, as *res et sacramentum*, has its own uniquely individual relation to her.[5] These findings as regards the

[2] H. Reiners, *Grundintention und sittliches Tun* (Freiburg–Basle–Vienna, 1966). Cf. P. Anciaux, *Das Sakrament der Busse* (Mainz, 1961); R. Blomme, *Widerspruch in Freiheit* (Limburg, 1965); P. Schoonenberg, *Theologie der Sünde* (Einsiedeln, 1966); L. Monden, *Sünde, Freiheit und Gewissen* (Salzburg, 1968). English edition: *Sin, Liberty and Law* (London/Dublin, 1966).

[3] B. Xiberta, *Clavis Ecclesiae* (Rome, 1922).

[4] C. Dumont, "La réconciliation avec l'église et la nécessité de l'aveu sacramental", in *Nouv. Rev. Théol.*, 81 (1959), pp. 577–97, esp. pp. 578–87.

[5] Cf. O. Semmelroth, *Die Kirche als Ursakrament* (Frankfurt/M., [2]1955);

Sacrament of Penance were not new—they had simply been rediscovered. They correspond to tradition and to Scripture, in which oneness with God is equated with oneness with the community of the chosen people, or as it may be, with the Church of Christ. Dumont notes that the relation of Penance to the Church should not be seen juridically, in the light of the schematic concept *res et sacramentum*, for this would be to misinterpret it. Incorporation into the Church is a living union with Christ.[6] Z. Alszeghy has made a closer assessment of this. He begins by rejecting the expression "reconciliation with the *Church*" on the ground that penance must always be directed towards *God*. Sin and repentance relate fundamentally to God. The Church is only the mediator and transmitter, not the end goal. Ultimately the Church does not reconcile men with herself but with God, whose presence within her is shown by "signs". For this reason Alszeghy prefers the description "return to peace with the Church", and uses as starting-point for his thesis the following sentence from Augustine: *"Ecclesiae caritas, quae per Spiritum Sanctum diffunditur in cordibus nostris, participum suorum peccata dimittit . . ."* This shows the Church as the community filled and sanctified with the love of the Holy Spirit. If, through repentance, we come once more into a personal relationship with the Church, we shall at the same time be at peace with God. For the Church is the presence of the eternal love of the Spirit of Christ, made visible in the faithful.[7] In a later essay K. Rahner asserts that Vatican II's Constitution on the Church concurred with Xiberta's thesis when it stated that the Sacrament of Penance brought about the reconciliation of the sinner with the Church. That is primary. The concept of *res et sacramentum* is secondary. Rahner then continues with an historical survey and justification of this long forgotten truth.[8] J. Ramos-Regidor notes the extent to which it has been granted world-wide recognition by

---

K. Rahner, *Kirche und Sakramente* (Freiburg/Br., 1960); E. H. Schillebeeckx, *Christus—Sakrament der Gottbegegnung* (Mainz, 1960). English edition: *Christ, The Sacrament* (London, 1963).

[6] *Op. cit.*, pp. 585–6.

[7] Z. Alszeghy, "Carità ecclesiale nella penitenza cristiana", in *Greg.*, 44 (1963), pp. 5–31.

[8] K. Rahner, "Das Sakrament der Busse als Wiederversöhnung mit der Kirche", in *Schriften zur Theologie VIII* (Einsiedeln, 1967), pp. 447–71.

the use the majority of distinguished contemporary professional theologians have made of it. Peace with the Church is the guarantee of peace with God.[9]

2. *Penance and the priesthood of the laity*

The entire Church's involvement in the forgiveness of sins came to be understood anew through the work of dogmatic historians, in particular B. Poschmann and K. Rahner. Theologians were then faced with the question of the actual part played by the universal priesthood and by the official priesthood. B. Langemeyer makes a very carefully considered attempt at an answer.[10] Following on the thought of M. Buber and F. Ebner, according to whom man only becomes truly himself through his relationship with others, he makes every Christian responsible for mediating salvation to his sinful fellow Christians. As against the Protestant view, particularly that of E. Brunner, that the power of forgiving sins belonged equally to all,[11] he concluded with Augustine that the community of the faithful, those filled with the love of the Holy Spirit of Christ, was indeed able to mediate the forgiveness of sins. But because, in its earthly existence, it was subject both to grace and sin, it needed an authentic priestly office through which the sinner would unfailingly know that forgiveness had truly been granted by all. For who could assert of himself with complete certainty that he possessed the Holy Spirit of Christ, which was able to forgive sins? According to B. Carra de Vaux Saint-Cyr, the division of function is as follows: The priest symbolizes Christ as head of the Church, and the faithful represent the people of God made one in the peace of the Church.[12] C. Jean-Nesmy

[9] J. Ramos-Regidor, "Il Sacramento della Penitenza, evento salvifico ecclesiale", in *La Penitenza* (*Quaderni di Rivista Liturgica* 9), Elle Di Ci (Torino–Leumann, ²1969), pp. 90–141, esp. pp. 110–14.

[10] B. Langemeyer, "Sündenvergebung und Brüderlichkeit", in *Catholica*, 18 (1964), pp. 290–314.

[11] For works from a Protestant standpoint on the Sacrament of Penance see L. Klein, *Evangelisch-Lutherische Beichte* (Paderborn, 1961); R. C. Gerest, "Renouveau de la confession privée et pensée des Réformateurs", in *Lumière et Vie*, 13 (1964), no. 70, pp. 122–36; B. Lohse, "Die Privatbeichte bei Luther", in *Kerygma und Dogma*, 14 (1968), pp. 207–28.

[12] B. Carra de Vaux Saint-Cyr, "Le mystère de la Pénitence: réconciliation avec Dieu, réconciliation avec l'Eglise", in *La Maison-Dieu*, 23 (1967), no. 90, pp. 132–54, esp. pp. 146–9.

sees the priest as the sacrament of Christ, and the people as the sacrament of the Church.[13] A. Turck cites many scriptural passages which, without particularizing, frequently speak of brotherly forgiveness; and he accords Christians the power of forgiving the sins of their fellows. But it is the bishops and priests who, together with the people, bring to active realization the mediating power of the whole Church.[14] All these theologians are of the view that the official priesthood gives added value to the priesthood of the laity. F. J. Heggen has his own theory. His starting-point is the "death of God" theology. He makes no distinction between love of God and love of neighbour, and considers that forgiving is the prerogative of the one who has been sinned against—one's fellow man. In this view sacramental confession is no more than a liturgical celebration in which the forgiveness granted in daily life reaches its high point. The essence of the Sacrament of Penance is the "making visible of a man's personal sinfulness in the presence of the community of the faithful, or perhaps the officially appointed representative of this community."[15] A. Eppacher agrees with this theory in a notable essay on the practice of general absolution during the ninth to the fourteenth centuries. For him the idea of penance as reconciliation with the Church was obscured by the equating of obligatory and devotional confession, for in the latter case it would not be possible to speak of a genuine return to peace with the Church. If we want to rescue the idea of devotional sacramental confession, we must seek for a definition of sacramentality in Heggen's sense, giving equal weight to both aspects—the repentant sinner, and his presence before the Church.[16] This concept of the Sacrament of Penance puts the official priesthood very much into the background—at any rate in theory. But we must not forget that in

[13] C. Jean-Nesmy, "L'éducation du comportement spirituel du pénitent", in *La Maison-Dieu*, 23 (1967), no. 90, pp. 189–208, esp. pp. 197–8.

[14] A. Turck, "L'église comme peuple de Dieu et le sacrement de pénitence", in *Paroisse et Liturgie*, 48 (1966), pp. 255–9.

[15] F. J. Heggen, *Gemeinsame Bussfeier und Privatbeichte* (Vienna, Freiburg, Basle, ²1967), item 75. English edition (re-edited): *Confession and the Service of Penance* (London, 1967).

[16] A. Eppacher, "Die Generalabsolution", in *Zeitsch. f. Kath. Theol.*, 90 (1968), pp. 296–308, 385–421, esp. pp. 416 ff. Eppacher quotes in support of his thesis H. B. Meyer, "Beichte und (oder) Seelenführung", in *Orientierung*, 11 (1965), pp. 133–8, esp. p. 136.

practice Eppacher is concerned with a strictly sacramental celebration of the forgiveness of venial sins, by means of a general absolution and without detailed confession, whereas Heggen refers serious public sins to the official priestly tribunal, possibly as a penitential measure.

3. *The Sacrament of Penance as liturgical celebration*

The rediscovery of the ecclesial dimension of Penance very soon revealed the liturgical poverty of private confession. Thus we note, in H. Manders and A. M. Roguet for example, the attempt to depict the community aspect of private confession in the light of the penances current in the early Church.[17] At the same time the non-sacramental celebration of penance as a community liturgy began to be propagated. It had already been practised, for pastoral reasons, in 1947–48, in a Belgian working-class parish. From there it spread, first to the adjoining countries, and then to the Christian Church as a whole.[18] In 1963 there appeared a collection of articles by Th. Maertens, E. Marcus and R. Blomme, under the descriptive title *Das Buss-sakrament ist eine Feier* [literally, The Sacrament of Penance is a Celebration.—Trans.]. The authors' principal object was to discuss the liturgical aspect of confession and to justify the public celebration of penance.[19] The teaching on the Sacrament of Penance was gradually being enriched by the idea which E. H. Schillebeeckx put forward on the subject of sacraments generally. Namely—that confession is a cultic act and therefore has an upward and downward aspect: the

[17] H. Manders, "Het Latijnse Biechtritueel", in *Tijdschrift voor Liturgie*, 44 (1960), pp. 279–301; A. M. Roguet, "Liturgische Zielzorg rond het Boetesacrament", *ibid*., pp. 314–22.

[18] For these celebrations, their development and the experiments associated with them, cf. R. Meurice, "Les célébrations de la pénitence", in *La Maison-Dieu*, 14 (1958), no. 56, pp. 76–95; Th. Maertens, "Analyse liturgique du sacrement de pénitence", in "La Pénitence est une Célébration", in *Paroisse et Liturgie*, 58 (Bruges, 1963), pp. 11–39, esp. p. 32; H. Blasche, "Andachtsbeichte oder öffentlichter Bussgottesdienst", in *Der Seelsorger*, 36 (1966), pp. 269–73; F. Sottocornola–L. Della Torre, *La celebrazione della penitenza nella comunità cristiana* (Brescia, 1966), esp. pp. 7–23; A. M. Roguet, "Les célébrations communautaires de la Pénitence", in *La Vie Spirituelle*, 49 (1967), pp. 188–202; M. Coloni, "Apprendre à célébrer la pénitence", in *La Maison-Dieu*, 23 (1967), no. 90, pp. 223–35.

[19] "La Pénitence est une Célébration", in *Paroisse et Liturgie*, 58 (Bruges, 1963).

community praising God, and God thereupon granting salvation.[20] Confession derives its twofold meaning of admitting one's sins and praising God from the Latin word *"confiteri"*. The penitent praises the just God who calls men to account, and the merciful God who forgives their sins.[21] In a very profound examination of the liturgy of Penance in the old *Pontificale Romanum*, W. Lentzen-Deis has discovered this same twofold aspect. The penitential act of confession is accomplished in two phases. The public confession of Ash Wednesday and that of Maundy Thursday signify acceptance of judgment and also forgiveness. They are praise of the God who is at once just and merciful.[22] But as confession is a liturgical act of prayer, it is related to the community. The community, together with the priest, intercedes for the repentant sinner, as happened so movingly in the early centuries.[23] The intercession of the community is actually still expressed in private confession today, in the prayers *Misereatur* and *Indulgentiam*,[24] and it has an important place in the liturgical celebration of Penance. According to E. Lipinski, the penitential ceremonies of ancient Israel were already, in essence, a liturgy of intercession.[25] The unconditional *"Ego te absolvo"* has only appeared since the Middle Ages. J. Ysebaert is convinced that the true rite of reconciliation of the first Christians is already to be found in the New Testament (1 Tim. 5. 22), and consisted in the episcopal laying on of hands, which was understood in the sense of authoritative intercession.[26] The Eastern Church has retained the "deprecatory" formula of absolution to

[20] Cf. E. H. Schillebeeckx, *op. cit.*

[21] See P. Anciaux–R. Blomme, *Beichten heute* (Mainz, 1964), p. 29 f. and 39; P. Jacquemont, "Des laics redécouvrent le sacrement du pardon", in *La Vie Spirituelle*, 49 (1967), pp. 525–31, esp. p. 528; A. M. Roguet, "Les célébrations communautaires", *op. cit.*, 191; J. Leclercq, "La confession, louange de Dieu", in *La Vie Spirituelle*, 50 (1968), pp. 253–65.

[22] W. Lentzen-Deis, *Busse als Bekenntnisvollzug*, Freiburg/Br., 1969.

[23] Cf. E. Marcus, "La pénitence publique", in *La Pénitence est une Célébration*, *op. cit.*, pp. 45–57, esp. pp. 53–6.

[24] See *inter alia* P. Anciaux–R. Blomme, *op. cit.*, pp. 46 f.; F. Funke, *Christliche Existenz zwischen Sünde und Rechtfertigung* (Mainz, 1969), pp. 100–4.

[25] E. Lipinski, *La liturgie pénitentielle dans la Bible* (*Lectio Divina*, 52) (Paris, 1969), esp. pp. 115–16.

[26] J. Ysebaert, "L'imposition des mains, rite de réconciliation", in *La Maison-Dieu*, 23 (1967), no. 90, pp. 93–102.

this day.[27] Thus it is not surprising that all three suggestions made in 1968 by the Liturgical Commission in Rome are in the "deprecatory" form, and that the laying on of hands by the priest is recommended as a visible sign of reconciliation.[28]

4. *The sacramental celebration of Penance*

If we truly believe that the Sacrament of Penance is a liturgical celebration involving the whole body of the Church, then we shall want the public celebration of Penance to be given full sacramental status. If we look on the matter in the light of the importance of our relationship to our fellow men, of the identification of love of God with love of neighbour, the value put upon the priesthood of the laity and active lay participation in the liturgy, and also with due regard to the Protestant point of view, then we shall be able to reduce the sacramental character of Penance, in common with F. J. Heggen, H. B. Meyer and A. Eppacher, to the following formula—the repentant sinner, in the presence of the Church. And thus we shall finally conclude, with Heggen, that the sacramental celebration of Penance can occur even without the official ministration of the priest.[29] Others follow the same line of thought, but in a more traditional framework. For true sacramentality they demand priestly absolution. But they no longer postulate the detailed confession of venial sins. L. Lieger justifies this practice by pointing to the Eastern Church in whose Office and eucharistic celebrations we find liturgical services of penance, which frequently conclude with a general absolution in the sacramental sense.[30] A. Eppacher also mentions as an equally possible

[27] L. Ligier, "Le sacrement de pénitence selon la tradition orientale", in *Nouv. Rev. Théol.*, 89 (1967), pp. 940–67, esp. pp. 949–51 (cf. the same article in Italian, "Il sacramento della Penitenza secondo la tradizione orientale", in *La Penitenza, Quaderni di Rivista Liturgica*, 9, *op. cit.*, pp. 145–75, esp. pp. 155–8). For confession in the Eastern Church see further L. Ligier, "Pénitence et Eucharistie en Orient", in *Orientalia Christiana Periodica*, 29 (1963), pp. 5–78; the same author's "Dimension personnelle et dimension communautaire de la pénitence en Orient", in *La Maison-Dieu*, 23 (1967), no. 90, pp. 155–88; Ph. de Regis, "Confession et direction dans l'Eglise orientale", in *Lumière et Vie*, 13 (1964), no. 70, pp. 105–21; K. H. Dalmais, "Le sacrement de Pénitence chez les Orientaux", in *La Maison-Dieu*, 14 (1958), no. 56, pp. 22–9.

[28] Cf. E. Siedlecki, "Renewing the Sacraments", in *Chicago Studies*, vol. 8, no. 1, Spring 1969, pp. 3–7, esp. p. 4.

[29] F. J. Heggen, *op. cit.*, pp. 75–6.

[30] See L. Ligier, "Dimension personnelle", *op. cit.*, pp. 164–86; the same

form of confession the general absolutions which were current during the Middle Ages in the West. These were generally regarded as having a sacramental character.[31] In addition the Church knew and knows emergency situations in which venial as well as mortal sins receive sacramental forgiveness without detailed confession.[32] This leads to the consideration that confession—which includes its judging aspect—was basically an act of faith, a personal encounter of the sinner with the merciful God. Thus it is less a question of a detailed admission of sins and far more—at least as regards venial sins—of a turning to God in faith and trust.[33] Many theologians are of the opinion that the needs of the majority of practising believers are met by the public celebrations of penance that have been advocated, since these believers are only rarely guilty of sins serious enough to lead to a complete turning away from God.[34] The Roman Liturgical Commission goes so far as to suggest that the sacramental character of these public celebrations of penance applies to all sins without exception, mortal sins included. These latter must of course be privately confessed later, but there is no longer the necessity for postulating a particular time, for example preceding the reception of Communion.[35]

5. *Penance and dialogue in the confessional*

In this crisis moment for confession the public celebration of penance need not entail the abolishment of the words used in the confessional. On the one hand many fear that communal celebrations of penance, with their public admissions of grave sins, would make obligatory confession impossible.[36] On the other hand private confession, with its personal guidance, contains so much positive good that its disappearance would be an irresponsible act on the part of the Church.[37] The present age with its frequently sensitive

author's "Le sacrement de pénitence", *op. cit.*, pp. 961–3 (in Italian, *op. cit.*, pp. 169–71.

[31] A. Eppacher, *op. cit.*, pp. 297–307.

[32] Cf. F. Funke, "Zur Sakramentalität der Bussfeiern", in *Diakonia*, 4 (1969), pp. 275–85, esp. p. 281.

[33] See L. Monden, *op. cit.*, p. 56.

[34] Cf. F. Funke, "Zur Sakramentalität", *op. cit.*, pp. 278–9.

[35] Cf. E. Siedlecki, *op. cit.*, p. 6.

[36] See among others L. Bertsch, "Busse und Beichte im Leben der Gemeinde", in L. Bertsch (editor), *Busse und Beichte* (Frankfurt/M., 1967), pp. 89–107, esp. p. 106.

[37] This is the view of G. Muschalek, "Beichte und geistliche Führung", in *Orientierung*, 29 (1965), pp. 161–4; J. Meyerschene, "Die pastorale

problems regarding man's moral life is in special need of the words of explanation and exhortation that are customary in the confessional. A general inquiry made in France in 1967 on the subject of confession revealed that many Christians valued the words spoken in the confessional for psychological reasons, and sought guidance as part of the reception of the sacrament.[38] Nowadays we are accustomed to expressing our views in a multiplicity of fields. But we still value, or have learnt once more to value, the possibility of private confession in which we are not overwhelmed with words, ourselves remaining anonymous—as sometimes happens in public celebrations of penance—but are given the opportunity to speak.[39] Z. Alszeghy has given his own explanation for the dialogue between priest and penitent—an explanation that may be of positive value to the development of confession. He assumes that absolution will ultimately be given before the actual confession. And the bare statement that the penitent must afterwards accuse himself of his sins seems to him altogether too formal and juridical. In the early Church confession was required for the purpose of imposing an adequate penance. In the Middle Ages it was thought necessary for making a true assessment of guilt before granting absolution. And now the confessing of sins might be thought of as the starting-point for the dialogue between priest and penitent, in which the latter would obtain the full fruits of forgiveness.[40]

6. *Penance in the entire spectrum of sacraments*

Within the seven sacraments Penance has a function of its own.

Bedeutung der häufigen Beichte", in *Anzeiger f.d. Kath. Geistlichkeit*, 76 (1967), pp. 92–102; "Über die gemeinschaftlichen Bussfeiern", in *Liturg. Jahrbuch*, 17 (1967), pp. 249–50. We read there of the intention of the French Liturgical Commission to ensure that the reform of the Sacrament of Penance does not do away with any of the possibilities for private confession. A. M. Roguet, "La confession des péchés véniels", in *La Maison-Dieu*, 23 (1967), no. 90, pp. 209–22; B. Dreher, "Sakramentale Bussformen", in *Leb. Seels.*, 19 (1968), pp. 31–6; F. Funke, *Christliche Existenz*, *op. cit.*

[38] Cf. C. Jean-Nesmy, "Les chrétiens parlent de la confession", in *La Vie Spirituelle*, 50 (1968), pp. 375–500, esp. pp. 388–9 and 464.

[39] Cf. R. Hostie, *Das Gespräch in der Seelsorge* (Salzburg, 1965); *Leb. Seels.*, 20 (1969), whose third number is entirely devoted to the topic *Das seelsorgerliche Gespräch* (*Pastoral Dialogue*), pp. 97–140.

[40] Z. Alszeghy, "Problemi dogmatici della celebrazione penitenziale comunitaria", in *Greg.*, 48 (1967), pp. 577–87, esp. p. 586.

Nevertheless the sacraments must be thought of as a totality. The forgiveness of sins does not only occur in the confessional. In fact it is Baptism that is ultimately the sacrament of repentance, and Penance the re-activation of the baptismal character which is always directed towards grace unless turned aside by grave sin.[41] The anointing of the sick is seen as the last earthly expression of penance.[42] And finally the Eucharist is once more moving closer to confession. L. Ligier notes that until the emergence of private confession, the Eastern Church had made only the three *"crimina"* of early Christian times subject to its own penitential discipline. All other sins, including those we should now consider grave, were forgiven during the eucharistic celebration. Thus he considers that two sacraments were combined in one liturgical celebration.[43] D. A. Tanghe points to the presence of real conviction, in East and West alike, of the Eucharist's power to forgive sins.[44] In J. M. R. Tillard's view Eucharist and Penance signify one single mystery of divine forgiveness, the Eucharist being primary. In the Eucharist, there must be no separation between Offering and Communion. Both appear under the same signs. The presence and power for salvation of the death and resurrection of Christ are evident here as nowhere else. Offering and Communion presuppose each other. Trent still showed awareness of this when it stated, *à propos* of the sacrifice of the Mass, that it "did away with sins and crimes, however grave" (cf. DS 1743, NR 514). The Fathers probably meant that if we partake of the Eucharist with the proper intention, we shall receive the grace of repentance and the capacity to receive Communion, as well as the inner disposition for subsequent confession, similar to the wish to receive the Sacrament of Penance which the sinner expresses, not because he is compelled but because he is impelled by love. The necessity of

[41] Cf. E. H. Schillebeeckx, "Het sacrament van den biecht", in *Tijdschrift voor Geestlijk Leven*, 8 (1952), pp. 219–42, esp. pp. 232–42; F. Funke, *Christliche Existenz*, *op. cit.*, pp. 80–1.

[42] See S. Zenker, "Vollendung der Busse. Gedanken zur Liturgie der Krankenölung", in *Anima*, 14 (1959), pp. 373–7.

[43] L. Ligier, "Pénitence et Eucharistie", *op. cit.*, pp. 65, 67 f., 71, 78; the same author's "Dimension personnelle", *op. cit.*, pp. 170–5; the same author's "Le sacrement de pénitence", *op. cit.*, pp. 958–60, 961–3 (in Italian, *op. cit.*, pp. 165–7, 169–71).

[44] D. A. Tanghe, "L'eucharistie pour la rémission des péchés", in *Irénikon*, 34 (1961), pp. 165–81.

confessing before receiving Communion is thus seen as solely a command of the Church. It cannot be deduced from the words of Paul (1 Cor. 11. 27). Within the total process of forgiveness, the Mass puts the emphasis on God, who reconciles all men to himself in Christ, and the Sacrament of Penance puts the emphasis on the decision of the sinner to return to the Father through Christ.[45] Thus A. Nocent would like to see the regulation about confession before Communion abolished in the Church, with the exception of grave public sins. He suggests that the penitential rite of the new *Ordo Missae* or perhaps the more meaningful public admission of guilt to be re-introduced after the liturgy of the word, the sermon and the Creed, should be declared a sacramental forgiveness of sin. Thus the sins of weakness that burden the conscience of the majority of communicants would no longer prevent them from receiving the Eucharist, which is an essential part of the Mass and often gives more strength to combat sin than a too frequent, legally enforced system of confession. Like Tillard, Nocent too requires a *votum sacramenti paenitentiae* which must be put into effect from time to time.[46]

7. *Different forms of Christian Penance*

Finally we note that Christian and ecclesiastical penance is not exhausted by the sacramental forms. Present-day scepticism about sacramental forms seems to be especially calculated to bring to expression the saving aspect of penance in all its various forms. W. Kasper, B. Dreher and F. Funke point to a rich field of possibilities for the forgiveness of sins, from the preaching and power of the word of God to lay confession, good deeds done, sufferings borne, and the public celebration of penance.[47] The sacramental

[45] J. M. R. Tillard, "Pénitence et eucharistie", in *La Maison-Dieu*, 23 (1967), no. 90, pp. 103–31; the same author's "L'eucharistie, purification de l'Eglise pérégrinante", in *Nouv. Rev. Théol.*, p. 84 (1962).

[46] A. Nocent, "L'acte pénitentiel du nouvel 'Ordo Missae': Sacrement ou sacramentel?", in *Nouv. Rev. Théol.*, 101 (1969), pp. 956–76, esp. p. 971; cf. the same author's "Problemi contemporanei sul sacramento della Penitenza", in *La Penitenza* (*Quaderni di Rivista Liturgica*, 9), *op. cit.*, pp. 9–24, esp. pp. 15–22.

[47] W. Kasper, "Confession outside the Confessional?", in *Concilium* (April 1967), pp. 17–22 (American edn., vol. 24); the same author's "Wesen und Formen der Busse", in *Katechetische Blätter*, 92 (1967), pp. 737–53,

form itself has its different gradations. Serious sins can be more or less serious. And in the same way obligatory confession can be divided, as J. H. Nicolas has it, into "confession of true conversion" and "confession after a fall". In the first instance we are dealing with a sinner who is returning to a new and positive way of life after prolonged turning away from God. And in the second, with someone who has only momentarily interrupted the general orientation of his life towards God.[48] Devotional confession could develop a visible double liturgy—that of private confession as it is practised now, and of public and sacramental celebration of penance. The Sacrament of Penance would thus do unique justice to the totality of human existence by transmitting to the Christian as an individual, and as a member of the community, the forgiving mercy of God.[49] The future of the Sacrament of Penance does not appear to lie in the abolishing of private confession but in a greater differentiation between Christian and ecclesial penance.[50]

---

esp. pp. 746–8; B. Dreher, *op. cit.*, esp. pp. 35–6; F. Funke, *Christliche Existenz, op. cit.*, pp. 189–93.

[48] J. H. Nicolas, "Tes péchés sont remis", in *La Vie Spirituelle*, 49 (1967), pp. 501–42, esp. pp. 510–12 and 516–21.

[49] Cf. F. Funke, *Christliche Existenz, op. cit.*, pp. 34–5 and 116.

[50] See H. Vorgrimler, "Das Buss-sakrament—iuris divini?", in *Diakonia*, 4 (1969), pp. 257–66, esp. p. 266.

Translated by Simon and Erika Young

PART III
DOCUMENTATION
CONCILIUM

Frans Heggen

The Service of Penance: A Description and Appreciation of Some Models

I. A General Outline of the Emergence of Services of Penance

JUST before the Second World War, Henri de Lubac published his book, *Catholicism. On the Social Aspects of Dogma*,[1] in which he said: "The efficacy of confession is explained in the same way as that of baptism. The bond between sacramental forgiveness and reacceptance into the community of the Church of the one who has separated himself from that community by his sin is no less clear in the case of the sacrament of penance. It is a disciplinary institution and an instrument of inner purification. Both of these aspects of the sacrament are not only connected with each other, but also, if I may express it in this way, closely united by the very nature of the matter. The early discipline made this natural bond emerge in a very striking manner. The whole outward process of public penitence and forgiveness showed very clearly that the reconciliation of the sinner is above all a reconciliation with the Church and that this reconciliation with the Church is, in turn, an effective sign of reconciliation with God."[2] This ecclesiological aspect of penance was, however, hardly expressed at all in the pastoral practice of private confession. In recent years, workers in the pastoral sphere have been actively looking for new possibilities, in a search that has to some extent been stimulated by a number of publications dealing with the

[1] Dutch edition, Utrecht and Antwerp (1952), based on the fourth French edition. English edition, London, 1950.

[2] *Op. cit.*, pp. 50–51.

history of this branch of theology.[3] All these workers share a feeling of impotence when confronted with a great number of individual penitents, finding it impossible to deal with each of them in a completely personal manner. They all say that very many Christians are hardly capable, and in many cases not at all capable of making a personal confession and that they tend to get no further than a list of a few points, frequently very stereotyped. There is consequently a prevalent feeling of unrest and a realization that it is necessary to give a communal form to penance. This is, as I have indicated, not a new phenomenon and, as early as the nineteen-fifties, French-speaking Catholics were discussing the possibilities of and even composing "communal services of penance",[4] intended primarily as a preparation for the sacrament of confession proper, which was itself maintained in its fixed ritual. It was said quite explicitly that there could be no question of "a sacramental absolution which is given simultaneously to several persons, apart from certain cases which are provided for under the law".[5] The texts of these early services were partly based on existing liturgical texts and a real attempt was made to give Christians a genuine moral education and thus to break through individualistic and infantile attitudes. Emphasis was placed not only on the communal character of human sin, but also on the correct attitude of the penitent and his personal orientation towards conversion. During the conference held at Vanves in 1958, a number of positive results were recorded. After careful preparation before the service, Christians celebrated together in a communal liturgical service which led to a deeper personal experience of *metanoia* and confession of guilt and which

[3] P. Anciaux, *La théologie du sacrement de pénitence au XIIe siècle* (Louvain, 1949); J. Grotz, *Die Entwicklung des Bussstufenwesens in der vornicänischen Kirche* (Freiburg, 1955); J. Jungmann, *Die lateinischen Bussriten in ihrer geschichtlichen Entwicklung* (Innsbruck, 1932); B. Poschmann, *Die Busse* (Freiburg, 1951); K. Rahner, *De poenitentia* (Innsbruck, [3]1955); T. Rast, *Von der Beichte zum Sakrament der Busse* (Düsseldorf, 1965); C. Vogel, *Le pécheur et la pénitence dans l'Eglise ancienne* (Paris, 1966); *ibid.*, *Le pécheur et la pénitence au Moyen-Age* (Paris, 1969).

[4] See D. Sauvage, *L'Eglise éducatrice des consciences par le sacrement de pénitence* (Paris, 1953); R. Meurice, "Les célébrations de la pénitence. Suggestions et expériences", in *La Maison Dieu*, 14 (1958), no. 56, pp. 76–95; T. Maertens, "Analyse liturgique du sacrement de pénitence", in *Paroisse et Liturgie*, 44 (1962), pp. 305–35.

[5] Meurice, *op. cit.*, p. 77.

at the same time also threw fresh light on and gave a new emphasis to the act of penance in its relationship with the Church. A further conclusion drawn from these experiences was that it might also be possible to include much larger numbers of people in group confessions: "It is estimated that, after this communal preparation, two or three times as many people could be included in confession, using the same number of priests as before".[6]

The Second Vatican Council gave encouragement to the continued development of this movement. The Constitution on the Sacred Liturgy contains, in paragraph 27, a plea for a communal form of service which should have the effect of stimulating the sense of being personally involved: "Whenever rites, in accordance with their very nature, need to be celebrated communally with active participation on the part of a great number of believers, it must be emphatically pointed out that this is to be given, as far as possible, priority over individual and, so to speak, private celebration. This applies especially to the celebration of the Mass, regardless of the public and social nature of each Mass, and to the administration of the sacraments."[7] The Constitution also had this to say about the sacrament of penance in particular: "The rites and the texts of the sacrament of penance must be revised in such a way that they express the nature and the effect of this sacrament more clearly".[8] In this, the Fathers of the Council were thinking especially of the communal character of the sacrament and its ecclesiological aspect. Pastoral theologians went even further in their investigations into the nature of the sacrament. It should be noted, however, in this connection, that those active in the liturgical movement have for a long time devoted almost all their attention to the celebration of the Eucharist and to Holy Week, Sundays and Lent. Penance has always been rather on the periphery as far as liturgists are concerned. It would seem as though there is such a great difference between the early practice of canonical penance and the contemporary practice of private confession that possibilities of finding modern forms of a service of penance which follow the practice of the early Church are hardly envisaged. This is, of course, to some extent because

[6] Meurice, *op. cit.*, p. 81.

[7] Vatican II, *Constitutio de sacra liturgia*, n. 27.

[8] *Ibid.*, n. 72.

scholars specializing in the liturgy have until very recently "concerned themselves almost exclusively with earlier liturgies, many of which had completely disappeared from practice, or with the liturgy which is officially prescribed by the Church in her liturgical books".[9] I personally have the impression that the scientific study of the liturgy has, until now, contributed too little to any real evaluation or creation of rites of penance which are adapted to contemporary needs.

In 1964, however, the Bishop of Roermond issued a number of guide-lines for use in his diocese in the matter of children's confession. These aroused a great deal of interest both in the Netherlands and abroad because they pointed out new ways and marked the beginning of a new stage in the study of the problem. Broadly speaking, the content of these guide-lines is as follows. The child should be introduced in phases to the sacrament of penance. It should begin, probably to a great extent unconsciously, in the family and the child's ordinary association with father and mother. It will continue in the stories told to the child about the goodness and love shown by God to man in Jesus Christ (and in all people who live according to his example). This introduction to the sacrament will become more conscious and more explicit when the theme of good and evil in man and the whole of creation is dealt with in prayer and song together with the children. The aim of this kind of instruction is to make the children's experience of wholeness and brokenness, of guilt and forgiveness, explicit, so that a climate can be gradually created in which the children can thank their heavenly Father—whom they discover again and again behind and in their parents and teachers—and ask his forgiveness, expressing this in a personal and suitable way. The child will approach the sacrament of penance itself in a communal celebration. In this way, the whole approach is gradual right as far as the reception of the sacrament itself and the child does not have to do very much himself or herself, as it were, or on his or her own. The introduction to the sacrament is completed when there is an opportunity for private confession alongside the communal service.[10]

[9] G. Lukken, "Vaticanum II en de liturgie", *Liturgisch Woordenboek, Supplement* (Roermond, 1970), p. 12.

[10] For a further discussion and elaboration of this question, see F. J.

The principle of a gradual introduction to the sacrament in phases has been generally accepted by most of those concerned, because it is in accordance with a practice which offers many advantages from the catechetical point of view. Anciaux and Bulckens in Belgium and Halbfass, Tillmann, Bertsch and Betz in Germany were among the first to favour this kind of introduction.[11]

Two main tendencies can be observed in the books and articles that have been published in recent years on the subject of penance. The writers who belong to the first of these movements advocate the integration of private confession into a communal service and they support this view with many arguments. They believe, for example, that the social aspects of sin and reconciliation as well as the ecclesiological dimension of the sacrament can be emphasized more strongly in this way. They also maintain that more attention can be given to deepening the penitent's insight into his own conscience in this combination of public service and private confession. Again, in this combination, confession and absolution would take place in the usual manner, the only difference being that personal contact between the penitent and the priest would take up much less time. The priest acts, in this case, more a minister of the Church than as a spiritual director—he simply accepts the penitent's personal, but very short confession of guilt and pronounces absolution. Because it takes place within the framework of the communal service of penance, the individual's going to the confessional must be done very quickly, otherwise too much time is taken up. Another argument that those in favour of this method put forward is that it is a service of *confession* which is fully in accordance with the definition of the Council of Trent that a precise confession must be made of all mortal sins committed.[12]

Heggen, *Intocht der kinderen* (Roermond, [3]1966), English translation, *Children and Confession* (London, 1969).

[11] P. Anciaux, *Het sacrament der boetvaardigheid* (Tielt and The Hague, [4]1965), p. 181; J. Bulckens, *Pastoraal en catechese van eerste biecht en eerste communie* (Antwerp, 1964); H. Halbfass, *Der Religionsunterricht* (Düsseldorf, 1966), p. 210; K. Tillmann, "Erstkommunion vor Erstbeichte", *Katholische Blätter*, 90 (1965), pp. 337–50; L. Bertsch, "Der rechte Zeitpunkt der Erst-Beichte", in *Stimmen der Zeit*, 175 (1965), pp. 225–62; O. Betz, "Umkehr und Beichte", *Katholische Blätter*, 90 (1954), pp. 202–8.

[12] See, for example, W. Bekkers, *Barmhartigheid en biecht*, St Michiels-

The second group consists of authors who, for practical and for ideal reasons, insist that a distinction should be made between two basic forms—the communal service of penance and private confession. I myself am in agreement with this. I very much doubt whether an integration of these two basic forms can be meaningful or even possible in the case of large groups of people and consequently cannot accept the arguments of the first group of theologians. (I have, incidentally, discussed this whole question in greater detail elsewhere.[13]) I am convinced, for example, that there is a great danger of haste. There is a danger that the confession itself will become no more than a general formula, with the result that personal expression is almost banished. There is, in such a communal service, no time for the priest to turn personally towards the penitent and to accept his confession in the true sense of the word. I find it rather strange that Coloni can speak at one point of a "private, secret and inter-personal dialogue"[14] and yet say, later in the same discussion, that the individual Christian is "deprived" of any personal choice of confessor, of place where the whole service, including confession, is to take place and, to some extent, also of his examination of conscience.[15] There is, in fact, hardly any real argument put forward by the members of this group in favour of integrating the communal service and private confession. They seem either not to realize that the two basic forms can be separated or to regard such a separation as impossible because of official pronouncements made by the Church.

The essential aspect of the sacrament of penance is to let the personal sinfulness of the penitent be seen by the community or by the qualified representative of that community. The Church's teaching office can in fact even direct that communal services in the strict sense of the word should be conducted. In a pastoral letter (16 March 1965), the Dutch bishops were very positive in their attitude towards the emergence of services of penance.

---

gestel (1963); M. Coloni, "Apprendre à célébrer la pénitence", in *La Maison Dieu*, 90 (1967), pp. 223–35; F. Sottocornola and L. della Torre, *La celebrazione della penitenza nella communità cristiana* (Brescia, 1966).

[13] F. J. Heggen, *Boeteviering en private biecht* (Roermond, [3]1966), English translation, *Confession and the Service of Penance* (London, 1967).

[14] Coloni, *op. cit.*, p. 230.

[15] *Ibid.*, p. 231.

It is precisely in such services that the social aspects of sin and penitence are fully stressed, since the Church is above all the place where guilt is confessed[16] and the proclamation of grace is communally accepted. In addition to this, however, private confession loses nothing of its value and it can also develop into a very personal expression and an intimate appropriation of Christ, even more, in fact, than it frequently could in the past. In this question, Alszeghy has interpreted the Tridentine canons concerned very casuistically and juridically and has, in my opinion, gone on wrongly to object to any possible recognition of the service of penance as a sacrament of the forgiveness of sins, including so-called "mortal sins".[17] I cannot unfortunately, because of lack of space, discuss his position in detail here. Partly on the basis of data drawn from the results of historical research, Funke clearly takes a relative view of Alszeghy's position.[18] Finally, Anciaux has stated explicitly: "The concrete form of the priest's ministry does not in itself determine the sacramental significance and extent of a rite. There can be no theological objection to recognizing this kind of service of penance as one of the expressions of sacramental conversion and reconciliation, on condition that a suitable accompaniment is found to the conversion and to reconciliation in the case of serious sins or to public abuses."[19]

II. Some Models of Services of Penance

A. Passion and Easter. A Service with Children[20]

If the meaning of this service is to be made quite clear to the children, we must already have spoken in class about the events that are to take place in it—darkness and light, passion and Easter. The more difficult task of explaining the meaning of the word "sin" may be attempted, but this depends on the age and development of the children.

[16] See, for example, D. Bonhoeffer's excellent chapter on this subject in his *Ethik* (Munich, [5]1961), pp. 46–54.

[17] Z. Alszeghy, "Problemi dogmatici della celebrazione communitaria", *Gregorianum*, 48 (1967), pp. 577–87.

[18] F. Funke, *Christliche Existenz zwischen Sünde und Rechtfertigung* (Mainz, 1969).

[19] P. Anciaux, *op. cit.*, p. 195.

[20] My thanks are due to the publishers, Gooi & Sticht, Hilversum, for permission to use this material here.

The service itself should take place in a quiet room or building, such as the church. In the sanctuary (if the church is used), a decorated cross is placed on the left and a lighted paschal candle on the right. Between them, there must be room for the priest and six children, who have been specially instructed beforehand, so that they know what to do during the service. The children who are not in the sanctuary sit down in the front pews of the church. Each child is given a candle. These small candles could have been decorated by the children before the service and could afterwards be given, for example, to the sick as an Easter gift. In any case, fruit or other gifts are brought forward by the children towards the end of the service, to be given later to the sick or other people.

The priest conducting the service comes with the six children from the sacristy. The six children light their candles from the paschal candle and form a semi-circle with the priest in the centre.

1. *The Priest's Opening Address*

We have come together today and are gathered round the cross and the candle because we belong to Jesus. It is his cross and it is his candle—his light. During Lent and especially on Good Friday, we think about how much Jesus suffered. Let us sing then—

2. *Song*

3. (*A Teacher now reads*, preferably from a children's Bible, such as that by J. Klink, *Bible for Children*,* New Testament, Volume II, the story of the death of Jesus (Matt. 27. 45–56; Mark 15. 33–39; Luke 23. 44–56), stressing the darkness which covered the earth when Jesus died. After this story, the paschal candle is extinguished and there is a short period of silence for personal prayer.)

4. *Priest*: It was dark. Not because of an eclipse of the sun, but because Jesus had been put to death—Jesus who was such a good man to everyone. This was very bad for his murderers and very bad for everyone. Every time a good man is murdered, the night comes—it becomes dark.

Think of America. It was a terrible pity about the murder of Martin Luther King. It was a terrible pity about the man who shot Robert Kennedy—very bad, a pity for him and very bad, a sin for

*London, 1967.

the whole of America, the whole of the world. Every time men do something very wrong, there is less light in the world. It becomes darker. It is a great pity, very bad, for the people who do wrong, and very bad, a sin for others. Listen to some stories about things that people do which are very bad for themselves and very bad, a sin, for others.

5. (*The six children* standing with their burning candles in a semi-circle around the priest now say, in turn, one of the following texts in a quiet but clear voice and emphatically.)
Child 1: Two nations live side by side. They ought to live together in peace, but they wage war. It is a terrible pity, very bad for those people. It is very bad, a sin, for the world. There is less light now in the world. (The child blows his or her candle out.)
All: Forgive us, Lord. We make the world dark around us.
Child 6 (the child standing on the outside of the semi-circle on the opposite side of Child 1): There are so many vegetables grown in our country, but the growers often say: "We can't get the prices we want" and throw the food away on dumps—while so many people are starving in the world. It is a terrible pity for the people who dump the food and it is very bad for the poor starving people, a sin. There is less light now. (The child blows his or her candle out.)
All: Forgive us, Lord. We make the world dark around us.
Child 2: An old man has been saving money all his life. Thieves break into his home and steal all his savings. It is very bad for the thieves and a sin, and very bad, for the old man. There is less light. (The child blows his or her candle out.)
All: Forgive us, Lord. We make the world dark around us.
Child 5: Two families quarrel. They can't stand each other. They are always upsetting each other and thinking the worst of each other. What a sin for those two families and what a pity for their friends. There is even less light. (The child blows his or her candle out.)
All: Forgive us, Lord. We make the world dark around us.
Child 3: A man makes his wife very unhappy. He has the chance to put it right again, but he doesn't do anything. What a pity. It is so bad for the husband and so bad for his wife. Even less light. (The child blows his or her candle out.)

All: Forgive us, Lord. We make the world dark around us.
Child 4: People often work terribly hard to make other people happy, but no one thinks of thanking them. How wrong of those other people and what a sin it is for all of us. Less light.... (The child blows his or her candle out.)
All: Forgive us, Lord. We make the world dark around us.

6. *Priest*: Boys and girls, all the candles are out now. There is much less light. It is darker all around us. When this happens, people feel miserable. They feel especially miserable when they know that it is their own fault—when they know that *they* have made the world dark around them and others. They are sorry about it. But it is never completely dark in the world around us, because Jesus' message to every person in the world is always there—whatever has happened, it is always possible to be forgiven.

7. *Song*

8. *Priest*: Let us now honestly confess our faults, our sins. Let us all tell God that we are sorry for the wrong things that we have done.
Confession of guilt: I confess to almighty God....

9. *Teacher*: Who will save us? Who will take away the darkness? Who will be the Light of the world? Who will help *us* to be light in the world? Listen to this Bible story about Jesus. (The teacher here reads, again preferably from a children's Bible, such as the *Bible for Children* by J. Klink, Volume II, the story of the meeting with Jesus on the road to Emmaus, Luke 24. 9–32, stressing the Christians' despondency after Jesus' death, then their hope and finally their certainty that he is with them. This story can also be enacted in mime by several of the children, again stressing the same elements. Finally, the paschal candle is lit again.)

10. *Priest*: The paschal candle is alight again—Jesus' death was not the end. He has risen again. He is alive! He brings light to all people. But he also says—Do as I did, do good to everyone and forgive other people who have done wrong things to you. Then God will forgive you as well. That is why I can, in the name of Jesus, say to you: May almighty God have mercy on you, forgive you your sins and bring you to everlasting life.

All: Amen.
Priest: May the almighty and merciful Lord grant you pardon, absolution and remission of your sins.
All: Amen.

11. *The six children* now say, in turn, one of the following texts and then light their candles again.
Child 1: Jesus is alive. He is the light of the world. Luckily there are people who hear his message and make the world light around them. (The child lights his or her candle again from the paschal candle and goes back to his or her place.)
All: Help us, Lord, to make the world light around us.
(During the following readings, a few children can enact what is said in simple mime—carrying a heavy load, helping mother, perhaps by washing up, in the family, reading to a blind person, doing first aid.)
Child 6: There are people who notice at once if someone else needs help—they run forward at once to help him carry a heavy load. They make the world light for others. (The child lights his or her candle from the paschal candle.)
All: Help us, Lord, to make the world light around us.
Child 2: There are people who like helping mother in a busy family. They get down to work straightaway. They are a light for others. (The child lights his or her candle.)
All: Help us, Lord, to make the world light around us.
Child 5: There are people who visit a blind person every week and read the newspaper aloud to him, so that he can have company and keep in touch with things. They bring light too. (The child lights his or her candle.)
All: Help us, Lord, to make the world light around us.
Child 3: There are people who give other people first aid, bandage their wounds, try to lessen their pain and to comfort them if they are depressed. They are a light for others in the world. (The child lights his or her candle.)
All: Help us, Lord, to make the world light around us.
Child 4: We have brought something here for sick people. (Children from the class bring a basket of fruit or other gifts or some decorations that they have made themselves.)
Child 4 (after having lit his or her candle): We want to make these people happy and bring a little light into their lives.

Priest: Boys and girls. Jesus wants his light to be spread further over the world. We can help to do that and we can show each other that we are going to help to spread Jesus' light over the world. Bring your candles forward now and receive the light of the paschal candle—Jesus' light.
(The whole class now comes forward from the pews. They form a large semi-circle, or several smaller semi-circles, opposite the semi-circle formed by the priest and the six children. The six children go with their lighted candles to the others and let them light their candles. They may, for example, say: "May your light shine everywhere." When all the candles are alight, the priest resumes.)
Priest: Children, Jesus will help us to be a light for others in the world around us, just as he was. He wants to give us something of his light. But he hopes that we will go out with that light, along the street, to school and home, to bring a little light wherever we can. Then Easter will be a really happy feast for us and for other people.

12. *Song* (the children may perhaps be able to sing verses that they have composed themselves on the theme of light).

Notes on this Service

This is, in my opinion, one of the best services of penance that I know which is especially composed for children and is available at present. The text is particularly well adapted to the needs of children—the point of departure is the child's concrete experience and the word of Scripture is placed within this context. The children are encouraged to take an active part in what is happening. The only negative criticism that I have is that the aspect of reconciliation is insufficiently stressed.

It is difficult to resist the temptation of comparing this service with other services of penance for children. In his *Zwanzig Bussfeiern mit Kindern*,[21] all of which are very biblical, Weber is guilty of several errors. In the first place, he is out of touch with the concrete experience of children. Secondly, the services are decidedly intellectual in content. Thirdly, the children are passive. There is no real liturgy. Dramatic and visual aspects are lacking.

Sottocornola provides what is little more than an outline. He

[21] Donauwörth, 1969.

makes little attempt to relate the liturgies with the concrete, everyday experience of the children and does not show the part played by the parents and teacher in wiping out guilt.

I too have tried my hand, years ago, at the composition of services of penance for children. My greatest difficulties were firstly to avoid a moralizing tone in the text and secondly to create a really liturgical event.[22]

B. A Service of the Sacrament of Penance and Forgiveness (composed by a group of theological students)

Opening Song

Greeting

Grace and peace be yours
from God our Father,
who has given men the power
to cure one another
and build each other up,
to absolve one another
and forgive each other
through the power of Jesus Christ.
(A short intermezzo follows, during which music can be played.)

I. *Recognition of our Sinfulness*

Brothers and sisters, we have come together here to celebrate the sacrament of penance, to hear the message of forgiveness after having come to realize and after having confessed that we are guilty, sinful people. One of man's earliest and deepest experiences is a sense of shortcoming, a sense that he is unable to do good. This leads to a sense of guilt. We do good, but we also do evil. There is no such thing as a guiltless man. There is only Pilate, repeated a million times—man trying again and again to wash his hands clean of guilt and failing. We know only too well that we are guilty, that we are sinful, but it is so difficult to express our sinfulness in words. How are we to confess our guilt honestly? Perhaps we shall see more clearly how we fall short if we look in the mirror that Jesus holds in front of us whenever he says who is, in his view, blessed. In these words, he tells us

[22] F. J. Heggen, *Children and Confession* (London, 1969). These services were written in collaboration with P. J. Mars.

how we ought to be. Let us therefore be quiet and relaxed, look at ourselves and listen to what he says:

1. How blessed are those who are poor as they stand before God and who do not imagine that they are strong without him.
2. Have we given any thought at all to our attitude towards God? Have we thought about him with trust, gratitude and love or have we been quite self-sufficient?
1. Blessed are those who show gentleness and courage and who resist without violence.
2. Are we free men and women who can change our point of view and who can listen to other people? Are we prepared to be tolerant and to be silent?
1. Blessed are those who accept human faults without bitterness, pain or regret.
2. Have we ever admitted that we are wrong and offered our apologies?
1. Blessed are those who stand up for right and justice—not for themselves, but for others.
2. Are we aware of people who are lonely or in distress and do we go forward to help them? Are we conscious of our duty towards the community, our duty to alleviate distress in the world? Have we made life impossible for others by talking too much? Have we really tried to live for other people or have we been living above all for ourselves—for our own comfort, our possessions and our pleasure? Are we selfish?
1. Blessed are those who forgive others and love them despite all their faults and shortcomings.
2. Do we hate and avoid certain people and refuse to speak to them? Do we forgive and forget? How do we behave towards our neighbours and all the people we meet every day? Are we separated from them by quarrels? Are we indifferent towards them?
1. Blessed are those whose intentions are pure and who are not seeking to advance themselves in their dealings with others.
2. Do we try to place ourselves above our fellow men? Are we liberal in our attitude, generously acknowledging the success of others without becoming envious? Have we made others suffer because of our own fault? Are we ready to admit our own faults?

1. Blessed are those who try to make peace where there is disagreement or division.
2. After a quarrel, do we wait for the other person to approach us or are we the first to attempt a reconciliation?
1. How blessed are those who are persecuted, reviled and mocked for Christ's sake, because they bear witness to him.
2. Does Jesus' good news play a real part in our lives? Are we open to the Spirit he wants to give us?
(A short period of silence; music may be played.)

II. *Where can we get with our evil?*
Reading from the Gospel: John 8. 1–12
Song
Short Address
Brothers and sisters, we have been thinking for a few moments about our own weakness. We have been looking in the mirror that Jesus holds in front of us and have seen the extent to which we fall short.

We should not, however, stand still here, thinking that it is enough simply to say that we fall short. Nor should we hide behind each other. That was not the reason why we came here this evening to take part in a service of penance. We must be prepared to declare that we are guilty with regard to our fellow men and with regard to God. We should have the courage to declare that we have done evil and have neglected to do good. Forgiveness of guilt, after all, begins with recognition of guilt. Recognition of guilt is in itself an invitation to forgiveness.

In the song that we have just sung, we said, "God, we are confused as we stand before you". In the reading from the Gospel that we have just heard, we learned how the Pharisees came to Jesus. They had caught a woman committing adultery. The law demanded that she should be killed by stoning. People seem to love to discuss among themselves who is bad and who is good. We love to stick a label on someone and then kill him or her stone-dead.

Jesus watches them come and looks at them. All that he says is: "If any one of you is without sin, let him throw the first stone." After that, he bends down and plays with the sand. There is a deathly silence. His words go home. One by one, beginning with the eldest, they go away. In this case, the eldest were probably those who were the wisest or those with the most dirt on their hands. "Woman, where are they?" Jesus asks. "Has no one condemned you? Then neither do I condemn you. Go away and sin no more."

Despite all sin and all evil, the future is made open here. A new opportunity is given. No one, nothing, is written off. This is something that should be deeply ingrained in our minds, because Jesus wants to redeem us so that we have this freedom. If we had known Jesus in person, if we had experienced this incident personally, then we should certainly have felt very confused.

God, we are confused as we stand before you. Jesus—he loved his enemies and forgave everyone in advance. His word of forgiveness is also bound to liberate us and enable us to make a new beginning. Where can we get with our evil? We can get to him, who tells us to forgive each other. Let us go to each other, then, and to him, who is different and who is love for all people.

He makes no difference beween people. He is faithful. He never lets a man go. He is true. In him, there is no yes and no—only yes. He is powerful, yet he serves man. His judgment is salvation and he does not want anything or anybody to be lost. That is why we may be bold enough to pray and to confess our guilt:

Confession of Guilt

I confess to almighty God,
to his saints and to all of you
that I have fallen short,
and I ask forgiveness
of all whom I have offended
and of all who have anything against me.
Have mercy on me, Lord God.

Prayer

Lord our God, whenever we are overwhelmed by the sense of our own evil, you make us aware of the contrasting power of your love. You call us to repentance and conversion and promise us reconciliation and peace, through Jesus your Son, in whom you are very close to us.

Absolve us and we shall pass the word of forgiveness on to one another, the forgiveness that we receive from him.

Place your hand on us whenever we fall and lift us up again, so that we shall go forward to help and serve each other and thus come closer to you. Amen.

Proclamation and Forgiveness

I can now proclaim the good news to you:

The Lord will have mercy on us, because he is greater than our hearts.

He has sent us his Son, not to condemn us, but to save us from fear and from death.

He forgives us our guilt and absolves us so that we may forgive each other.

And his power will bring about a new creation in us, so that we become different people.

Amen.

(The celebrant then stretches his hands out over the people and prays:)

May God, who brings salvation, have mercy on you.

May he show you his compassion and take away all your sins.

And may almighty God, the Father, the Son and the Holy Spirit, bless you and remain with you always. Amen.

(The processional cross, with a candle on each side, is now carried down the central aisle. The people may be sprinkled with holy water. A song is sung.)

Dismissal (based on 1 Pet. 3. 8–9)

Finally, brothers and sisters, be all of you of one mind in sympathy, brotherly love, mercy and humility. Do not repay evil with evil and do not revile those who revile you. On the contrary, bless each other so that you may inherit the blessing to which you have been called, the blessing of the Father, the Son and the Holy Spirit. Amen.

Concluding Song

C. A Service of Penance as a Preparation for Easter
(composed by a group of priests engaged in pastoral work)

1. *Opening*

May the grace of the Lord Jesus Christ, the love of God and the fellowship of the Holy Spirit be with you all (2 Cor. 13. 13).
Amen.

Brothers and sisters, we have come together here to prepare ourselves for Easter. We cannot celebrate this feast until we have straightened everything out with God and with our fellow men. In this service of penance, then, we shall confess to God and our fellow men that we have often not fulfilled the expectations that God and our fellow men may have had of us. But God is always ready to grant us forgiveness whenever we honestly admit our faults.

God is, after all, merciful to all who look to him in trust. May we therefore all be ready to grant forgiveness to each other. Our very presence here is already a confession of guilt.

May this deepen our repentance and turn us to joy and gratitude. In this service of penance, we hope to be able to stand aloof for a little while from the many cares and worries of our everyday lives. In the light of Jesus, we hope that we shall be able to see our situation in life more clearly—that it could have been better. With the help of this honest self-examination, we shall be able to approach Easter and its joy as new, glorified people. Amen.

2. *Opening Song*

3. *First Reading* (all sit)
Psalm 32; Gal. 6. 1–10; Col. 3. 12–17

4. *Gradual*

5. *Second Reading* (all stand)
Matt. 5. 1–12; John 3. 16–21

6. *Reflection about our Lives* (all sit)
We are all conscious of our lack of love. Every day we realize that we do not come up to expectations. That is why there is so much hatred, hardness and dishonesty and so little trust and understanding in our world. In our own world—that is, in our own country, in our own parish, in our immediate environment and in ourselves. In our sphere of work, we are always encountering misunderstandings. We are quick to criticize, but we often forget that we ourselves work among those people and are also responsible for what takes place there.

In our family life too, relationships are not always as they should be. There are days of indifference and there are days of tension.

Among our friends and acquaintances, we find that we are often slow to come forward to meet each other. Our good intentions often have the wrong effect. Without wanting to, we misunderstand each other. We are often suspicious. We treat unimportant things too seriously. We sometimes let ourselves be too much influenced by an unpleasant first impression. Frequently we simply refuse to see other people's good qualities and achievements. This all results in misunderstanding, a lack of love....

We insist on our own rights through thick and thin. We refuse to speak to certain people—our parents, our children, a member of our own family, a neighbour, someone at work. We just walk past them. We embarrass each other by what we say or write. We are intolerant and blind to other people's distress, to their loneliness, their illness, their poverty and their hunger.

We often treat each other like numbers, not like people at all—people who need affection and sympathy. We often try to make use of other people by fine promises and by abusing our position, by flattery, charm or false sympathy, even by bribery. We are all guilty. Not one of us is free of guilt....
(Silence)

7. *Prayer for Forgiveness*

Brothers and sisters, let us now pray together for forgiveness—we talk too much about love, but practise it too little.

All: Forgive us, Lord. (This is repeated after each intention.)

We denigrate others and do not respect their opinions.

We are not able honestly to forgive others and to live with each other's faults and shortcomings.

In our dealings with one another, we often lose sight of what is only of relative importance in life and have too little sense of humour.

We are guilty of coarse language and boasting.

We are often so possessive.

We so often place ourselves in the centre of things and everything and everybody has to revolve around us so that there is no room left in our lives for our fellow men.

We sometimes compel others to accept our point of view and always want to be in the right.

Let us pray: Lord, we often fall short in our contacts with our fellow men. We often cause each other to suffer unnecessarily or else ignore each other. It is always very difficult to change course once we have set off in the wrong direction. That is why we ask you, Lord, to forgive us and to give strength to those whom we have treated wrongly, for the sake of our unity in Jesus Christ.

8. *Confession of Guilt*
Let us now confess our guilt very honestly.
I confess to almighty God . . .
May almighty God have mercy on us, pardon our sins and bring us to everlasting life. Amen.
May the almighty and merciful Lord grant us pardon, absolution and remission of our sins. Amen.

9. *Song of Praise*

10. *Prayer of Thanksgiving and Bidding Prayers*
Let us now thank God together and entrust everything to him in hope, in particular everything that touches our hearts.
God, our Father, we thank you that you are a God of people and that you forgive us in your goodness every time that we sin.
All: We thank you, God. (This is repeated after each intention.)
We thank you for all your good gifts—for the patience that you have with us, for the love with which you surround us every day of our lives and for everything that you have done among us through Jesus Christ, your Son.
We thank you for life and health, for the bread on our table, for the house we live in and for all the things that we enjoy every day and that we are responsible for subject to you.
We thank you for your Church—despite her faults and shortcomings. You have given us your Church to be a visible sign of your salvation here on earth and something that we can hold on to in our journey towards you.
We thank you for this opportunity to be together here in this service of penance. Remembering that you have told us to pray without ceasing, however, we want especially to commend these people to you—everyone living on this earth, young or old, belonging together and going through life together, people of all races and nations, but especially those near to us: the people who live in our parish, our family, neighbours and friends and acquaintances and those who are closest of all to us, as close as our own body: our husband, our wife, our parents, our children and

all who are entrusted to our care. May we continue to try to understand and love each other so that we may be happy together. Our Father . . .

11. *Dismissal*

Brothers and sisters, through our faith we have been granted forgiveness of our sins. We are at peace with God through our Lord Jesus Christ. Soon we shall be celebrating together our feast of Easter. It is a feast that promises us that we can rise out of our littleness and it is also the beginning of our real life with God, which commences with our life here on earth.

Now we shall go our different ways, renewed and at peace with each other. We shall in the future try to behave with modesty because we know how imperfect we are and with courage because we have Christian hope. We shall try to bring love where there is hatred, forgiveness where guilt, and faith where doubt. Let us try to be really human towards each other. Then there will be peace among us, the peace of Easter, and our lives will be pleasing to God, whose name I now invoke upon you in blessing —the Father, the Son and the Holy Spirit. Amen.

Notes on Services B and C

Both of these services have proved to be good in practice. Many priests and lay people have reacted favourably towards them. All the same, I find them only partly successful. Service C is rather strongly moralizing in tone and it corresponds too closely to the tendency to which Lukken refers "to let liturgical language deteriorate into descriptive, instructive or intellectual talk. In the liturgy, we are after all concerned above all with the basic words of Christian existence, in other words, with a confessing, proclamatory, evocative and orientating way of speaking."[24] Service B has a directness which makes a clear appeal to religious experience. The symbolism is weak, especially in the case of Service C. Perhaps the authors of the texts have not been daring enough— the language they use is not sufficiently evocative.

[24] G. Lukken, "De ontwikkeling van de liturgie sinds Vaticanum II", in *Liturgisch Woordenboek, Supplement*, p. 22.

Translated by David Smith

Biographical Notes

JEAN-JACQUES VON ALLMEN was born 29 July 1917 at Lausanne and ordained in the Reformed Church in 1941. He studied at the Universities of Lausanne, Basle and Neuchâtel. Doctor of theology, he is professor of practical theology at the University of Neuchâtel. His publications include *Prophétisme sacramentaire* (Neuchâtel, 1964) and *Essai sur le repas du Seigneur* (Neuchâtel, 1966).

CHRISTIAN DUQUOC, O.P., was born 22 December 1926 at Nantes and ordained in 1953. He studied at the Dominican Studium of Leysse (France), the University of Fribourg, the Faculties of the Saulchoir (France) and the Biblical School of Jerusalem. A lecturer and doctor in theology, with a diploma of the Biblical School of Jerusalem, he is professor of dogmatics at the Faculty of Theology of Lyons (since 1957) and a member of the editorial committee of *Lumière et Vie*. His publications include *L'Eglise et le Progrès* (Paris).

FELIX FUNKE, of the Picpus Fathers, was born 14 July 1932 at Velen, Kreis Borken (Germany) and ordained in 1959. He studied at the Gregorian University, Rome. Doctor of theology, he is lecturer in theology at the Collegium Damianeum of Simpelveld (Netherlands). His publications include *Christliche Existenz swischen Sünde und Rechtfertigung* (Mainz, 1969).

JAMES MCCUE was born 7 January 1931 at Chicago. He is a Catholic. He studied in the U.S.A. at Loyola University (Chicago) and the University of Wisconsin. Master of arts and doctor of philosophy, he is assistant professor of positive theology at the University of Iowa. His publications include "The Roman Primacy in the Second Century and the Problem of the Development of Dogma", in *Theological Studies* (1964).

HARRY MCSORLEY, C.S.P., was born 20 December 1931 at Philadelphia and ordained in 1960. He studied in the U.S.A. at Bucknell University and St. Paul's College, Washington, and in Germany at the Universities of Heidelberg and Tübingen. Master of arts and doctor of theology, he is professor of ecumenical and ecclesiological theology at St Paul's College, Washington. His publications include *Luthers Lehre vom unfreien Willen* (Munich, 1967).

FRANZ NIKOLASCH was born 3 April 1933 at Millstatt/See (Austria) and ordained in 1958. He studied at the Gregorian (Rome). Licentiate in philosophy and doctor of theology, he is professor of liturgy at the University of Salzburg. Among his publications is *Das Lamm als Christussymbol in den Schriften der Väter* (Vienna, 1963).

CARL PETER was born 4 April 1932 at Omaha and ordained in 1951. He studied in Rome at the Angelicum and the Gregorian. Doctor of philosophy and of theology, he is associate professor of systematic theology at the Catholic University of America at Washington. Among his publications is *Participated Eternity in the Vision of God* (Rome, 1964).

JOSÉ RAMOS-REGIDOR, S.D.B., was born 10 October 1930 at Banos de Montemayor (Spain) and was ordained in 1959. He studied at the University of Salamanca and at the Salesian Athenaeum in Turin. Licentiate in philosophy and doctor of theology, he is professor of dogmatics and of systematic theology at the Salesian Athenaeum in Rome. His publications include *Signo y poder. A propósito de la exégesis patrística de Jn 2. 1–11* (Rome, 1966).

JEAN REMY was born 14 November 1928 at Soumagne (Belgium). He studied at the University of Louvain. Licentiate in philosophy and doctor of economic sciences, he is director of studies at the Faculty of political and social sciences at the University of Louvain and director of the Centre of socio-religious researches (*section francophone*) at the same university. Among his publications are: *Charleroi et son agglomération*, 2 vols. (Louvain, 1961) and *Famille et relations personnelles en milieu urbain* (Paris, 1965).

JEAN-MARIE TILLARD, O.P., was born 2 September 1927 at Iles Saint-Pierre et Miquelon. He studied at the Angelicum (Rome) and at the Saulchoir (France). Doctor of philosophy and master of theology, he is professor of dogmatics at the Faculty of Theology in Ottawa. Among his publications is *Le sacrement, évènement du salut* (Brussels, 1964).

D0110080

MERCYHURST COLLEGE
HAMMERMILL LIBRARY
ERIE, PA 16546